The Spanish Teacher's Resource Book

Lesson Plans, Exercises, and
Solutions for First Year Spanish Class

By
Stephen Jackson
M.A.

Dedication

This book is dedicated to my friend and former master teacher, Juan "Guapo" Mora. When I was a rookie teacher he showed me, through word and example, what to avoid in my choosen profession and what to embrace and foster. All of this was packaged both in seriousness and an unmatched sense of humor. This beautiful man who had the priviledge of working with Ceasar Chavez himself, has since retired from teaching. However, he continues to teach and continues to be a noted community leader. He will always be a passionate advocate for educators and for the advancement of our distinguished enterprise. Gracias, Guapo.

Acknowledgements

To my wife Caroline and son Liam, thanks for your enthustiastic support and encouragement for this project. Knowing that you were in my corner even when I hit rough patches in writing made all the difference. Whatever flaws there are in this volume are mine and mine alone.

To the Teacher

This book is written for middle and high school Spanish teachers. The subject matter covers material normally taught in first year Spanish classes.

There are 7 chapters and 30 lessons. Each lesson is designed to stand on its own and comes with its set of exercises and their solutions. There are 39 exercises, most of them 20 items or more.

In addition, you will find a verb bank of regular verbs, a verb bank of reflexive verbs, a listing of popular activities, a pronunciation guide and two appendices.

Each exercise comes with its solutions. This enables you to select either a particular lesson you wish to teach or a suite of related topics.

Each lesson is preceded by its objective, its method of accomplishment, and its outcome so that your students know what is expected from the start. Since the concepts underlying the lessons are explained in some detail and are backed by examples, your students can be challenged to explain the basic concepts in each leson and even produce examples of their own either through group or individual work. Activities such as these allow you to make accessments more easily and target areas that merit greater attention.

I hope you find this book useful. I enjoyed

writing it and I hope it brings you satisfaction, if not some pleasure using it.

      I need your comments, both positive and negative, so I can continue what's good and eliminate, or strengthen, this book's weaker points. Send your comments to: ***griot1017@gmail.com***

      Be fearless! Thanks.

Contents

Part 1

How to Conjugate Regular Verbs in the Present Indicative

Six Key Terms

Objective: Learn 6 key terms used in conjugation.
Method: Practice defining key terms orally or in writing.
Outcome: Explain 5 key terms orally or in writing using your own words.

We **conjugate in order to tell who is doing what and when**.The *when* refers either to the present, past,or future. In this lesson we conjugate verbs so that we can speak and write in the present.

Key Terms
    Verb: Belongs to a class of words that represent actions, for example, *to run*, or a state, for example *to be* or *to exist*.
    The Present Indicative: This term describes when a verb is used to make a factual statement or used to ask a question in the present as opposed to the past or future. For example:
    -*El hombre es alto*. (The man is tall).

    -*¿Dónde está el Parque Balboa*? (Where is Balboa Park?)
    An Infinitive: A basic form of the verb that, by itself, gives no reference to past, present, or future time. The marker for the infinitive in English is *to* which preceeds the verb as in *to*

speak, to eat, to live.

Spanish verbs are divided into 3 classes, those with **-ar** endings, those with **-er** endings, and those with **-ir** endings. These endings are known as **infinitive endings**. For example:

    habl**ar** = to speak
    com**er** = to eat
    viv**ir** = to live

The Stem (or root) of a Spanish Verb: This is the infinitive minus its **ar**, or **er**, or **ir** ending. For example:

    Habl**ar** → habl
    com**er** → com
    viv**ir** → viv

The stem of *hablar* is **habl**, the stem of *comer* is, **com**, and the stem of *vivir* is **viv**.

The inflected endings. There are 3 sets of inflected endings for regular Spanish verbs in the Present Indicative tense. When these inflected endings are correctly attached to the stems of regular verbs, they tell us **who** or **what** is performing an action and **when** that action is taking place.

The inflected endings are laid out in *Figure 1* below.

Number	-ar Verbs	-er Verbs	-ir Verbs
Singular	-o -as -a -a	-o -es -e -e	-o -es -e -e
Plural	-amos -áis -an -an	-emos -éis -en -en	-imos -ís -en -en

Fig. 1

Number tells us whether there is one or more than one person or thing performing an action. The **singular** inflected endings are used when we talk or write about **1person or thing**. The **plural** inflected endings are used when we talk or write about **2 or more persons or things**.

You will now see how all these terms apply when we conjugate regular verbs in the present indicative in the 3 sections that follow.

Exercise: Key Terms

1. Why is conjugating a verb important?
2. How can you identify an infinitive in English? Give an example.
3. How can you identify an infinitive in Spanish? List 1 example of each of the 3 types of Spanish verbs.
4. What is the stem (or root) of a Spanish verb? Give an example.
5. What does *number* refer to in Spanish grammar? Give 2 examples.
6. What are inflexional endings? Select inflexional endings from either –ar or -ir verbs and list them.
7. Inflexional endings are important because

   _____.

8. What is an infinitive ending? Give 3 examples.
9. Explain **why** the following statements are in the present indicative:
   The dogs run on the beach.
   Why are you here?

Exercise Solution: Key Terms

1. Why is conjugating a verb important?
    Conjugating a verb tells us who or what is
    performing an action and when.

2. How can you identify an infinitive in
    English? Give an example. In English the
    infinitive is preceded by the word to. An
    example: *to study*.

3. How can you identify an infinitive in
    Spanish? List 1 example of each of the 3
    types of Spanish verbs. The Spanish
    infinitives end with –ar, -er, and –ir. Three
    examples are: *montar*, t*emer*, and *vivir*.

4. What is the stem (or root) of a Spanish verb?
    Give an example. The stem of a Spanish
    verb is what remains after the infinitive
    ending is dropped. Example: salt*ar* → salt

5. What does *number* refer to in Spanish
    grammar? Give 2 examples. It refers to
    whether a noun or pronoun is singular, or 1
    or whether a noun or pronoun is plural, 2 or
    more. Example, the car, singular referring to
    1 car; the cars, plural referring to 2 or more
    cars.

6. What are inflexional endings? Select
    inflexional endings from either -*ar* or -*ir*
    verbs and list them. Inflexional endings are
    what we add to the stems of verbs when we
    conjugate them.

Here are the inflexional endings for *-ar* verbs:

Singular: *o*, *as*, *a*, *a*

Plural: *amos*, *áis*, *an*, *an*

7.   Inflexional endings are important because <u>when correctly attached to the stems of verbs, they tell us **who** or **what** is performing an action and **when** that action is taking place</u>.

8.   Spanish verbs are divided into 3 classes with either *-ar* endings, or *-er* endings, or *-ir* endings. These endings are known as infinitive endings.

9.   Explain *why* the following statements are in the present indicative:

The dogs run on the beach.

Why are you here?

Because in the first sentence, the verb is used to make a factual statement and is in the present. The next item is a question also in the present, as opposed to the past or future.

How to Conjugate Regular *-ar* Verbs in the Present Indicative

Objective: Learn how to conjugate a regular -*ar* verb in the present indicative.
Method: Memorize a model -*ar* verb.
Outcome: Explain how to change any regular -*ar* verb from its infinitive form to its conjugated form to its use in a sentence.
When a regular -*ar* verb is unconjugated, it is in its infinitive form and looks like this: **tomar**. When that same verb is conjugated it looks like this:

Singular
1. yo tom**o** = I drink

2. tú tom**as** = you (fam.) drink

*3. él/ella tom**a** = he/she/it drinks
4. usted tom**a** = you (form.) drink

Plural

†5. nosotros tom**amos** = we drink

6. vosotros tom**áis** = you drink

+7.ellos/ellas tom**an** = they drink.

 8. ustedes tom**an** = you drink

Key to symbols in conjugation above

* = The name of 1 person or 1 thing can replace *él/ella* in position 3 above. Example: *John toma agua*. (John drinks water).

† = Whenever the phrase …*y yo* (…and I) occurs, use the verb in position 5 above. Example: *Susie, Paula y yo tomamos agua*. (Susie Paula <u>and I</u> drink water).

\+ = The name of 2 or more persons or 2 or more things can replace *ellos/ellas* in position 3 above. Example: *John y Anita toman agua*. (John drinks water). *Los gatos toman leche*. (The cats drink milk)

Three steps in conjugating an -ar verb

There are 3 basic steps in conjugating an *ar* verb:
    1. **Drop the infinitive ending** of *tomar*

    2. **Keep the stem** *tom*.

    3. **Add the present indicative endings** for *ar* verbs:
    Singular *o*, *as*, *a*, *a*

    Plural *amos*, *áis*, *an*, *an*

that match what you wish to say or write.
For example if you wish to say, *I drink Pepsi Cola*, it would be: *Yo tomo Pepsi Cola*. Similarly, for *We*

drink lemonade, it would be: *Nosotros tomamos la limonada*.

There are many regular *-ar* verbs with the same endings as **tomar** when they are conjugated. Some of them are: **hablar**, **montar**, **bailar**, **saltar**, and **mirar**.

Exercise: Conjugate *ar* Verbs

Fill in the blanks with the correct form of the present indicative by correctly conjugating the *ar* verb in parentheses. What you fill in must correctly match the underlined nouns or pronouns.

1. <u>Yo</u> (apagar) _____ la luz.
2. <u>Nosotros</u> (nadar) _____ en el mar.
3. <u>Ellas</u> (tomar) _____ agua.
4. <u>Él</u> (dibujar) _____ un retrato.

5. <u>Tú</u> no (fumar) _____ los cigarillos.
6. <u>Ella</u> (saltar) _____ del tren.
7. <u>Usted</u> (marchar) _____ los lunes.
8. <u>Maria, Andy, y yo</u> (andar) _____ por la calle.
9. <u>Ustedes</u> (tirar) _____ basura.
10. <u>Ellos</u> (llorar) _____ en casa.
11. *Juan y Mario* (pagar) _____ la multa.
12. *Nosotras* (comenzar) _____ el concurso.
13. *Roberto* (hablar) _____ con ella.
14. *Tú* no (viajar) _____ a México.
15. <u>El perro y yo</u> (pasar) _____ un buen tiempo.
16. <u>Vosotros</u> (borrar) _____ el pizarrón.
17. <u>Miguel</u> (ganar) _____ diez dólares.
18. <u>Los estudiantes</u> (mirar) _____ la foto.

19.   <u>Chris, Patricio, y Ahn</u> (escuchar)

_____música.

20.   <u>El pájaro</u> (cantar) _____en el árbol.

Exercise Solution: Conjugate *-ar* Verbs

1. Yo (apagar) <u>apago</u> la luz.
2. Nosotros (nadar) <u>nadamos</u> en el mar.
3. Ellas (tomar) <u>toman</u> agua.
4. Él (dibujar) <u>dibuja</u> un retrato.
5. Tú no (fumar) <u>fumas</u> los cigarillos.
6. Ella (saltar) <u>salta</u> del tren.
7. Usted (marchar) <u>marcha</u> los lunes.
8. Maria, Andy, y yo (andar) <u>andamos</u> por la calle.
9. Ustedes (tirar) <u>tiran</u> basura.
10. Ellos (llorar) <u>lloran</u> en casa.
11. Juan y Mario (pagar) <u>pagan</u> la multa.
12. Nosotras (comenzar) <u>comenzamos</u> el concurso.
13. Roberto (hablar) <u>habla</u> con ella.
14. Tú no (viajar) <u>viajas</u> a México.
15. El perro y yo (pasar) <u>pasamos</u> un buen tiempo.
16. Vosotros (borrar) <u>borráis</u> el pizarrón.
17. Miguel (ganar) <u>gana</u> diez dólares.
18. Los estudiantes (mirar) <u>miran</u> la foto.
19. Chris, Patricio, y Ahn (escuchar) <u>escuchan</u> música.
20. El pájaro (cantar) <u>canta</u> en el árbol.

How to Conjugate Regular -*er* Verbs in the Present Indicative

Objective: Learn how to conjugate a regular -*er* verb in the present indicative.
Method: Memorize a model -*er* verb.
Outcome: Explain how to change any regular -*er* verb from its infinitive form to its conjugated form to its use in a sentence.

When a regular -*er* verb is unconjugated, it is in its infinitive form and looks like this: ***comer***.
When that same verb is conjugated it looks like this:

Singular

1. yo com**o** = I eat

2. tú com**es** = you (fam.) eat

*3. él/ella com**e** = he/she/it eats.

 4. usted com**e** = you (form.) eat

Plural

†5. nosotros com**emos** = we eat

6. vosotros com**éis** = you eat

+7. ellos/ellas com**en** = they eat.

8. ustedes com**en** = you eat

Key to symbols in conjugation above

* = The name of 1 person or 1 thing can replace *él/ella* in position 3 above. Example: *John come el helado*. (John eats ice cream).

† = Whenever the phrase ...y yo (...and I) occurs, use the verb in position 5 above. Example: *Susie, Paula y yo comemos papas fritas*. (Susie Paula and I eat French fries).

+ = The name of 2 or more persons or 2 or more things can replace *ellos/ellas* in position 3 above. Example: *John y Anita comen pizza*. (John and Anita eat pizza). *Los gatos comen el pan*. (The cats eat bread).

<u>*Three steps in conjugating an -er verb*</u>

There are 3 basic steps in conjugating an *-er* verb:
    1. **Drop the infinitive ending** of *comer*
    2. **Keep the stem** *com*.
    2. **Add the present indicative endings** for *er* verbs:
Singular: *o, es, e, e*

  Plural: *emos, éis, en, en*

that matches what you wish to say or write.
For example if you wish to say, *She eats fruit*, it would be: *Ella come la fruta*. Similarly, for *You eat hamburgers*, it would be: *Ustedes comen las hamburguesas*.

There are many regular *-er* verbs with the same endings as **comer** when they are conjugated. Some of them are: **beber**, **aprender**, **correr**, **creer**, and **vender**.

Exercise: Conjugate -er Verbs

Fill in the blanks with the correct form of the present indicative by correctly conjugating the *er* verb in parentheses. What you fill in must correctly match the underlined nouns or pronouns.

1. Ellas (leer) _____ muchos libros.
2. Yo no (vender) _____ mi carro.

3. Manolo (correr) _____ dos kilómetros.

4. Usted (hacer) _____ la tarea.

5. Anita, Pablo y yo (aprender) _____ francés.

6. Él no (beber) _____ Coca Cola.

7. Nosotros (tener) _____ la pluma.
9. Gabby y yo no (querer) _____ nada.
10. Vosotros (perder) _____ la pelota.
11. Señor Robles (comer) _____ el flan.
12. Ella no (creer) _____ en Dios.

13. Tú no (leer) _____ el periódico.

14. Ellos (esconder) _____ mis llaves.
15. Rosalinda (meter) _____ el libro en mi mochila.
16. El chico (romper) _____ el vaso.

17. Tú no (temer) _____ la noche.

18. Yo (poseer) _____ la casa roja.

19. Él no (prometer) _____ nada.

20. Vosotras nos (deber) _____ veinte

dólares.

Solution to Exercise: Conjugate *-er* Verbs

Fill in the blanks with the correct form of the present indicative by correctly conjugating the *er* verb in parentheses. What you fill in must correctly match the underlined nouns or pronouns at the start of each sentence.

1. Ellas (leer) leen muchos libros.
2. Yo no (vender) vendo mi carro.

3. Manolo (correr) corre dos kilómetros.

4. Usted (hacer) hace la tarea.
5. Anita, Pablo y yo (aprender) aprendemos

francés.

6. Él no (beber) bebe Coca Cola.

7. Nosotros (tener) tenemos la pluma.
9. Gabby y yo no (querer) queremos nada.

10. Vosotros (perder) perdéis la pelota.

11. El Señor Robles (comer) come flan.
12. Ella no (creer) cree en Dios.

13. Tú no (leer) lees el periódico.

14. Ellos (esconder) esconden mis llaves.
15. Rosalinda (meter) mete el libro en mi mochila.
16. El chico (romper) rompe el vaso.

17. Tú no (temer) temes la noche.

18. <u>Yo</u> (poseer) <u>poseo</u> la casa roja.

19. <u>Él</u> no (prometer) <u>promete</u> nada.

20. <u>Vosotras</u> nos (deber) <u>debéis</u> veinte dólares.

How to Conjugate a Regular *-ir* Verb in the Present Indicative

Objective: Learn how to conjugate a regular *-ir* verb in the present indicative.
Method: Memorize a model *-ir* verb.
Outcome: Explain how to change any regular *-ir* verb from its infinitive form to its conjugated form to its use in a sentence.

When a regular *-ir* verb is unconjugated, it is in its infinitive form and looks like this: ***vivir***.
When that same verb is conjugated it looks like this:

Singular
1. yo viv**o** = I live

2. tú viv**es** = you (fam.) live

*3. él/ella viv**e** = he/she/it lives

4.usted viv**e** = you (form.) live

Plural

✝5. nosotros viv**imos** = we live

6. vosotros viv**ís** = you live

+7.ellos/ellas viv**en** = they live

8. ustedes viv**en** = you live

Key to symbols in conjugation above

* = The name of 1 person or 1 thing can replace *él/ella* in position 3 above. Example: *John vive en Madrid*. (John lives in Madrid).
† = Whenever the phrase …y yo (…and I) occurs, use the verb in position 5 above. Example: *Susie, Paula y yo vivimos en la casa verde*. (Susie, Paula, and I live in the green house).
+ = The name of 2 or more persons or 2 or more things can replace *ellos/ellas* in position 3 above. Example: *John y Anita viven en Calle Ocho*. (John and Anita live on Eight Street). *Los perros no viven en el salón de clase*. (The dogs do not live in the classroom).

Three steps in conjugating an -ir verb

There are 3 steps in conjugating an *-ir* verb:
    1. **Drop the infinitive ending** of *vivir*
    2. **Keep the stem** *viv.*

    3. **Add the present indicative endings** for *er* verbs:
Singular *o*, *es*, *e*, *e*

    Plural **emos**, **ís**, **en**, **en**

that match what you wish to say or write.
For example if you wish to say, *She lives in Australia*, it would be: *Ella vive en Australia*. Similarly, for *We live in New York*, it would be:

Nosotros vivimos en Nueva York.

There are many regular *-ir* verbs with the same endings as **vivir** when they are conjugated. Some of them are: **abrir**, **escribir**, **insistir**, **decidir**, and **recibir**.

Exercise: Conjugate -*ir* Verbs

Fill in the blanks with the correct form of the present indicative by correctly conjugating the *er* **verb in parentheses.** What you fill in must correctly match the underlined nouns or pronouns at the start of each sentence.

1. Nosotros (abrir) _____ la puerta verde.
2. Ustedes (escribir) _____ muchas cartas.
3. Anita (vivir) _____ en Korea.
4. Perla y Andy (compartir) _____ los tacos.
5. Pablo y yo (subir) _____ las escaleras.

6. Yo no (admitir) _____ la verdad.

7. Usted (asistir) _____ la escuela secundaria.
8. Las chicas (descubrir) _____ una planta nueva.
10. La cuerda (unir) _____ los dos partes.
11. El sombrero (cubrir) _____ la cabeza.
12. Vosotras (omitir) _____ la pregunta.

13. Tú no (existir) _____ en el año 1558.

14. Carlos (describir) _____ Rosalinda.

15. Mi tía (recibir) _____ el regalo.

16. El cura (partir) _____ el pan en dos.

17. Tú y yo (decidir) _____ entre dos deportes.

18. Él (sufrir) _____ mucho.

19. Ellos no (permitir) _____ la fiesta.

20. Mario y yo (discutir) _____ las diferencias entre la lluvia y la nieve.

Solution to Exercise: Conjugate *-ir* Verbs

Fill in the blanks with the correct form of the present indicative by correctly conjugating the *-er* verb in parentheses. What you fill in must correctly match the underlined nouns or pronouns at the start of each sentence.

1. Nosotros (abrir) abrimos la puerta verde.
2. Ustedes (escribir) escriben muchas cartas.
3. Anita (vivir) vive en Korea.
4. Perla y Andy (compartir) comparten los tacos.
5. Pablo y yo (subir) subimos las escaleras.
6. Yo no (admitir) admito la verdad.
7. Usted (asistir) asiste a la escuela secundaria.
8. Las chicas (descubrir) descubren una planta nueva.
10. La cuerda (unir) une los dos partes.
11. El sombrero (cubrir) cubre la cabeza.
12. Vosotras (omitir) omitís la pregunta.
13. Tú no (existir) existes en el año1558.
14. Carlos (describir) describe Rosalinda.
15. Mi tía (recibir) recibe el regalo.
16. El cura (partir) parte el pan en dos.
17. Tú y yo (decidir) decidimos entre dos deportes.

18. Él (sufrir) sufre mucho.

19. Ellos no (permitir) permiten la fiesta.

20. Mario y yo (discutir) discutimos las diferencias entre la lluvia y la nieve.

Verb Bank: Regular Spanish Verbs

-ar Verbs

1. alquilar - to hire, rent
2. amar – to love
3. andar - to walk
4. ayudar – to help
5. bailar - to dance
6. buscar – to look for
7. cantar - to sing
8. cocinar – to cook
9. comprar - to buy
10. contestar – to answer
11. dejar - to leave
12. desear – to desire
13. entrar - to enter
14. enviar – to send
15. enseñar - to teach
16. escuchar – to listen to
17. esperar - to wait, hope for
18. estudiar – to study
19. firmar – to sign
20. ganar - to win
21. gastar – to spend money
22. hablar - to speak, talk
23. lavar – to wash
24. llegar - to arrive
25. llevar – to carry
26. mirar – to watch
27. mandar - to send, order
28. olvidar - to forget
29. pagar – to pay
30. practicar - to practice
31. quitar – to remove
32. preparar - to prepare
33. regresar – to return
34. saludar - to greet
35. saltar – to leap, jump
36. tocar – to touch, play(an instrument)
37. tomar - to take, drink
38. trabajar – to work
39. viajar - to travel
40. visitar – to visit

-er Verbs

1. aprender - to learn
2. beber – to drink

3. barrer - to sweep   4. comer - to eat
5. compeler - to compel   6. cometer - to commit
7. entender – to understand
8. correr - to run
9. conceder - to concede, grant, award
10. creer – to believe
11. deber - to have to, owe
12. depender - to depend
13. esconder – to hide   14. leer – to read
15. meter en - to put into
16. poseer – to possess, own
17. proceder - to proceed
18. prender - to switch on, grab, seize
19. prometer - to promise
20. romper – to break
21. temer - to fear   22. vender – to sell

-ir Verbs

1. abrir - to open   2. admitir – to admit
3. asistir - to attend
4. cubrir – to cover   5. cumplir – to complete
6. combatir - to combat
7. descubrir - to discover
8. discutir – to argue 9. escribir - to write
10. existir – to exist   11. insistir - to insist
12. omitir - to omit   13. dividir – to divide
14. permitir - to permit 15. pulir - to polish
16. recibir – to receive
17. subir - to climb, go up
18. sufrir – to suffer   19. unir - to unite
20. vivir – to live

Part 2

Five Key Irregular Verbs in the Present Indicative

Five Key Irregular Verbs in the Present Indicative

An irregular verb is one that does not follow the expected pattern for a verb in its class. For example, *ser* is an *-er* verb and if we drop its infinitive ending and tried to conjugate it, our first entry would, logically, be *yo so*. This would be wrong, however, because the first correct entry is *yo soy*. The irregularity does not stop there because the second entry for *ser* is *tú eres* which means that for some irregular verbs, even the stem changes.

Spanish has many irregular verbs but the most common for beginning learners are: **ser** *(to be)*, **estar** *(to be)*, **ir** *(to go)*, **hacer** *(to do, to make)*, and **tener** *(to have)*. Since these verbs do not follow regular patterns, they should be memorized.

How to Conjugate and Use Irregular Verb *Ser* (to be) in the Present Indicative

Objective: Learn how to conjugate the irregular verb *ser* in the present indicative.
Method: Memorize *ser,* say it, write it out.
Outcome: Change *ser* from its infinitive form to its conjugated form. Use it correctly in exercises that follow.

Singular
1. yo soy = I am

2. tú eres = you are (familiar)

*3. él/ella es = he/she/it is

 4. usted es = you are (formal)

Plural
†5. nosotros somos = we are
6. vosotros sois = you are
+7.ellos/ellas son = they are
 8. ustedes son = you are

*, †, + *See Appendix A on Page 281 on what these symbols mean.*

How Ser Is Used

Although *ser* and *estar* mean the same thing, (*to be*), when translated into English, they are used quite differently. Here are 7 common uses of ser:
1. When paired with an adjective *it expresses an inherent quality* not likely to change.
–*Ana es inteligente* (*Ana is smart.*)
 –*Roberto es alto.* (*Roberto is tall.*)

2. It is used *with de to indicate origin*
–La familia Robles es de Argentina (The Robles family is from Argentina.).

 – Miguel y su mamá son de Las Vegas. (Miguel and his mom are from Las Vegas.)

3. To indicate *what something is made of*
–*La mesa es de Madera. (The table is made of wood.).*
– *El carro es de acero. (The car is made of steel.)*

4. With *professions, nationality, and religious membership*.

–*Su papá es médico* (Her dad is a doctor.)

Yo soy pescador. (I am a fisherman.).
- *Nosotros somos mexicanos* (We are Mexican.)

 Tú eres panameño. (You are Panamanian.)

–*Ali es musulmán* (Ali is Muslim.)

María y Magdalena son Católicas. (Mary and Magdalena are Catholic.)

5. With **Generalizations**.

–*La amistidad es importante* (Friendship is important.)

–*Los números son útiles*. (Numbers are useful.)

6. Talking about **time of day.**

–*¿Qué hora es*? (What time is it?)

–*Es la una* (It's one o'clock.)
–*Son las doce y media* (It's twelve thirty.)

7. Talking about **where and/or when an event takes place.**

–*La reunión es el lunes*? (The meeting is on Monday.)

–*La fiesta es en el parque a la una* (The party is in the park at one o'clock.)

Exercise: Conjugate *Ser*

Fill in the blanks with the correct form of the present indicative by correctly conjugating the verb *ser* in parentheses. What you fill in must correctly match the underlined nouns or pronouns at the start of each sentence.

1. La chica (ser) _____ alta.

2. Ellos no (ser) _____ cómicos.

3. Tú (ser) _____ serio.

4. Miguel (ser) _____ mi amigo.

4. Yo no (ser) _____ trabajador.

6. Ariel y yo (ser) _____ hermanos.

7. Usted (ser) _____ estudiante.

8. Los chicos (ser) _____ morenos.

9. Los pájaros (ser) _____ verdes.

10. Nosotros (ser) _____ timidos.

11. Ustedes no (ser) _____ profesores.

12. Miguel y Jenny (ser) _____ bajos.

13. Vosotras (ser) _____ de Madrid.

14. Mi papá no (ser) _____ de Bolivia.

15. Las galletas (ser) _____ ricas.

16. (Ser) _____ las dos y cinco.

17. Las papas fritas (ser) _____ amarillas.

18. El número de teléfono (ser) _____ 224- 6807.

19. Javier y yo (ser) _____ inteligentes.

20. El helado (ser) _____ de chocolate.

Solution to Exercise: Conjugate *Ser*
Fill in the blanks with the correct form of the present indicative by correctly conjugating the verb *ser* in parentheses. What you fill in must correctly match the underlined nouns or pronouns at the start of each sentence.

1. La chica (ser) es alta.

2. Ellos no (ser) son cómicos.

3. Tú (ser) eres serio.

4. Miguel (ser) es mi amigo.
4. Yo no (ser) soy trabajador.
6. Ariel y yo (ser) somos hermanos.
7. Usted (ser) es estudiante.
8. Los chicos (ser) son morenos.

9. Los pájaros (ser) son verdes.

10. Nosotros (ser) somos timidos.
11. Ustedes no (ser) son profesores.
12. Miguel y Jenny (ser) son bajos.
13. Vosotras (ser) sois de Madrid.

14. Mi papá no (ser) es de Bolivia.

15. Las galletas (ser) son ricas.
16. (Ser) Son las dos y cinco.
17. Las papas fritas (ser) son amarillas.

18. El número de teléfono (ser) es 224-6807.

19. Javier y yo (ser) somos inteligentes.
20. El helado (ser) es de chocolate.

How to Conjugate and Use Irregular Verb *Estar* in the Present Indicative

Objective: Learn how to conjugate the irregular verb *estar* in the present indicative.
Method: Memorize *estar,* say it, write it out.
Outcome: Change *estar* from its infinitive form to its conjugated form. Use it correctly in exercises that follow.

Singular
1. yo estoy = I am

2. tú estás = you (fam.) are

*3. él/ella está = he/she/it is

 4.usted está = you (form.) are

Plural
†5. nosotros estamos = we are

6. vosotros estáis = you are

₊7.ellos/ellas están = they are

 8. ustedes están = you are

*, †, + *See Appendix A on Page 281 on what these*

symbols mean.

How Estar Is Used

Although *ser* and *estar* mean the same thing, (*to be*), when translated into English, they are used quite differently. Here are 4 common uses of *estar*:
1. When paired with an adjective *it expresses a temporary condition or state* likely to change.
–*Estamos enfermos hoy.* (We are sick today.)

–*Ellos están enfadados con Arturto.* (They are angry at Arturo.)

2. *It indicates location*.

–*La mochila está en mi casa* (The backpack is in my house.)

–*Los Angeles y San Diego están en California.* (Los Angeles and San Diego are in California.)

3. When the present indicative of *estar* is paired with the present participle of a verb, it forms the present progressive tense for *ongoing action*.
(See more detail on pages 53 - 54).
–*Mi hermano y yo estamos corriendo.* (My brother and I are running.)

–*La muchacha está abriendo la ventana.* (The girl is opening the window.)

4. Used with para and the infinitive *it expresses to be about to and the infinitive*.

–*Estamos para escuchar música* (We are about to listen to music.)

 –*Yo estoy para salir a pasear. (I am about to leave for a walk.)*.

Exercise: Conjugate *Estar*

Fill in the blanks with the correct form of the present indicative by correctly conjugating the verb *estar* in parentheses. What you fill in must correctly match the underlined nouns or pronouns at the start of each sentence.

1. Los hombres (estar) _____en la tienda.
2. Juan y yo no (estar) _____ cansados.
3. Mi tío (estar) _____ bien hoy.
4. Profesores Castillo y Montes (estar) _____ en mi clase.
5. Yo no (estar) _____ trabajando.
6. Nosotros (estar) _____ en Paris.
7. Ustedes (estar) _____ encantados con la

música cubana.

8. La bicicleta (estar) _____ en el
gimnasio.

9. ¿Dónde (estar) _____ Argentina?

10. Yo (estar) _____ en el parque.
11. La bicicleta (estar) _____ en la clase de
Susana.
12. Los muchachos (estar) _____ enfermos.
13. Ella (estar) _____ en Chicago.

14. Mi libro y lápiz (estar) _____ debajo
del escritorio.

15. Él no (estar) _____ en la playa.

16. Mi primo (estar) _____ cantando ahora.

17. Claudia (estar) _____ triste hoy.

18. David, ¿dónde (estar) _____

Adela y tú?

19. Yo (estar) _____ bien, gracias.

20. Mauricio y yo (estar) _____ para comer tacos de pescado.

Solution to Exercise: Conjugate *Estar*

Fill in the blanks with the correct form of the present indicative by correctly conjugating the verb *estar* in parentheses. What you fill in must correctly match the underlined nouns or pronouns in each sentence.

1. Los hombres (estar) <u>están</u> la tienda.

2. <u>Juan y yo</u> no (estar) <u>estamos</u> cansados.

3. <u>Mi tío</u> (estar) <u>está</u> bien hoy.

4. <u>Profesores Castillo y Montes</u> (estar) <u>están</u> en mi clase.

4. <u>Yo</u> no (estar) <u>estoy</u> trabajando.

6. <u>Nosotros</u> (estar) <u>estamos</u> en Paris.

7. <u>Ustedes</u> (estar) <u>están</u> encantados con la música cubana.

8. <u>La bicicleta</u> (estar) <u>está</u> en el gimnasio.

9. ¿Dónde (estar) <u>está</u> Argentina?

10. <u>Yo</u> (estar) <u>estoy</u> en el parque.

11. <u>La bicicleta</u> (estar) <u>está</u> en la clase de Susana.

12. <u>Los muchachos</u> (estar) <u>están</u> enfermos.

13. Ella (estar) está en Chicago.

14. Mi libro y lápiz (estar) están debajo del escritorio.

15. Él no (estar) está en la playa.

16. Mi primo (estar) está cantando ahora.

17. Claudia (estar) está triste hoy.

18. David, ¿dónde (estar) están Adela y tú?

19. Yo (estar) estoy bien, gracias.

20. Mauricio y yo (estar) estamos para comer tacos de pescado.

The Present Progressive

Objective: Learn how to form and use the present progressive.

Method: Outline the process of combining *estar* and the present participle to form the present progressive.

Outcome: Demonstrate mastery of the present progressive by correctly performing exercises that follow.

In Spanish the present progressive is used to describe an action performed right now. It is made up of two parts:

(a)The conjugated verb *estar* (to be)

Singular

1. yo estoy = I am

2. tú estás = you are (familiar)

3. él/ella está = he/she/it is

4. usted está = you are (formal)

Plural

5. nosotros estamos = we are

6. vosotros estáis = you are

7. ellos/ellas están = they are

8. ustedes están = you are

(b)The present participle. In English the present participle is easily recognized because it ends with the letters -*ing*. Examples of present participles are: *talking, walking, eating*, and *studying*.

To form the present participle in Spanish for verbs ending in *ar*, drop the *ar* ending and add **ando**.
     Habl*ar* → habl → habl**ando**

To form the present participle in Spanish for verbs ending in *er*, drop the *er* ending and add **iendo**.
     beb*er* → beb → beb**iendo**

To form the present participle in Spanish for verbs ending in *ir*, drop the *ir* ending and add **iendo**.
     viv*ir* → viv → viv**iendo**

To form the present progressive, put items from **(a)** and **(b)** together in that order. For example, if you wish to say I am eating (now), select the correct part of the conjugated verb estar and add it to the present participle of the verb comer (to eat).
     Yo estoy comiendo. = I am eating.
Similarly, with the verb hablar (to speak)

     Ellos están hablando. = They are talking.

Exercise: Present Progressive

Do the following:

A.   Form the present participle of the verbs that follow.

Model: bailar →bail**ando**

   Salir → sal**iendo**

   1. saltar
   2. mirar
   3. brillar
   4. juntar
   5. escribir
   6. comprender
   7. abrir
   8. volver
   9. tomar
   10. correr

B.   Write out the present progressive for each of the verbs above by using the following pronouns in this order:

1. yo 2. tú 3. el/ella   4. usted

5. nosotros 6. vosotros 7. ellos 8. ustedes

Model: bailar → Yo estoy bail**ando.**

   Salir → Ustedes están sal**iendo.**

making sure to use each part of the conjugated verb *estar* at least once.

C.   Translate each of your present progressives above into English.

Model: Yo estoy bailando. = I am dancing.

Ustedes están saliendo. = You are leaving.

Solutions to Exercise: Present Progressive

Do the following:

A.   Form the present participle of the verbs that follow.

Model: bailar →bail**ando**

Salir → sal**iendo**

1. saltar →   saltando
2. mirar → mirando
3. brillar →   brillando
4. juntar → juntando
5. escribir → escribiendo
6. comprender → . comprendiendo
7. abrir →   abriendo
8. volver → volviendo
9. tomar →   tomando
10. correr → corriendo

B.   Write out the present progressive for each of the verbs above by using the following pronouns in this order:

1. yo 2. tú 3. Él/ella   4. Usted

5. nosotros 6. vosotros 7. ellos 8. ustedes

Model: bailar → Yo estoy bail**ando.**

Salir → Ustedes están sal**iendo.**

1. saltar →   Yo estoy saltando.

2. mirar → Tú estás mirando.

3. brillar → Ella está brillando.

4. juntar → Usted está juntando.

5. escribir → Nosotros estamos escribiendo.

6. comprender → Vosotros estáis
comprendiendo.

7. abrir → Ellos están abriendo.

8. volver → Ustedes están volviendo.

9. tomar → Yo estoy tomando.

10. correr → Tú estás corriendo.

C. Translate each of your present progressives
above into English.
Model: Yo estoy bailando. = I am dancing.

   Ustedes están saliendo. = You are leaving.

1. Yo estoy saltando. = I am jumping.

2. Tú estás mirando. = You are looking.

3. Ella está brillando. = She is shining

4. Usted está juntando. = You are
joining.
5. Nosotros estamos escribiendo. = We are
writing.

6. Vosotros estáis comprendiendo. = You are understanding.

7. Ellos están abriendo. = They are opening

8. Ustedes están volviendo. = You are returning.
9. Yo estoy tomando. = I am drinking/taking.

10.Tú estás corriendo. = You are running.

Comparing the Uses of Ser and Estar

Objective: Learn how to differentiate the use of _ser_ and _estar_.

Method: Study and discuss the key differences between these two verbs using lesson material.

Outcome: Show you have mastered the key points of difference between _ser_ and _estar_ by correctly completing the exercise that follows.

In English there is but one version of the verb _to be_. In Spanish there are two: _ser_ and _estar_.

Ser is used to communicate permanence such as a trait or characteristic not subject to change.

Estar is used to express temporary conditions subject to change over time. (The _notable exception_ is **estar muerto** = to be dead. _Su bisabuelo está muerto_ = His great grandfather is dead.)

Figures 2 and 3 provide a convenient usage summary along with examples.

Uses of Ser

Nationality and where from	*El amigo de Ana es cubano pero ella es de San Diego.* (Ana's friend is Cuban but she is from San Diego.)
Profession	*Mis hermanas son enfermeras.* (My sisters are nurses)
Characteristics of people or things	*Pedro es alto.* (Pedro is tall.) *El mar es enorme.* (The sea is enormous)
To ask/say what people are like	*¿Cómo es Irma?* (What is Irma like?) *Irma es muy inteligente.* (Irma is very smart.)
Possession	*El vestido es de Monica. ¿De quién es la camiseta? Es de Miguel.* (It is Monica's dress. Whose T-shirt is it? It is Miguel's)
What an object is made of	*La regla es de madera pero las botellas son de plástico.* (The ruler is made of wood but the bottles are of plastic.)
Hour and date	*Son las tres y media de la tarde. Hoy es jueves, el veinte de junio.* (It is 3:30 p.m. Today is Thursday, June 20.)
Where and when an event takes place	*El desfile es en el parque. Es domingo a las nueve de la mañana.* (The parade is in the park. It is on Sunday at nine in the morning.)

Fig. 2

Uses of Estar

Location,	*Los estudiantes están en la biblioteca.* (The students are in the library.)
To ask/say where people are	*¿Dónde está Julio?* (Where is Julio?) *Julio está* en el carro. (Julio is in the car)
Physical condition	*El suelo está limpio.* (The floor is clean.) *La manzana está verde.* (The apple is unripe.)
Emotional states	*Estoy emocionante porque ganó mi partido.* (I'm excited because my team won.)
Health	*Mi abuela está enferma pero mi abuelo está bien.* (My grandmother is sick but my grandfather is well.)
Ongoing actions in progressive tenses	*Carmen está practicando el baile antes de su quinceañera mañana.* (Carmen is practicing the dance before her quinceanera tomorrow.)
With adjectives to express sensory impression	*La ceda está lisa.* (The silk feels smooth.) *Maribel está guapa hoy.* (Maribel looks pretty today.)
Results of previous action (with past participles)	*El gimnasio está cerrado.* (The gym is closed.) *Las sillas están rotas.* (The chairs are broken.)

Fig. 3

Exercise: Uses of Ser and Estar

Select either ser or estar by underlining the items that follow:

1. Los Angeles es / está en California.

2. --¿Cómo está / es usted hoy, señora Morales?—

   --Bien, gracias.--

3. ¿Qué hora es / está?

4. Los estudiantes están / son trabajadores.
5. Las tiendas son / están abiertas durante la noche.
6. La bicicleta es/ está de acero.
7. La fiesta está / es en apartamento de Carolina.

8. —¿De dónde eres / estás tú? —

   — Yo soy / estoy de Guatemala.—
9. Los zapatos están / son de Carlos.
10. Vosotras sois / estáis furiosas porque sale ella.
11. David y yo estamos / somos hablando.
12. Mario es / está abogado y es / está muy serio.
13. Marisol y Beatriz son / están enfermas hoy.

14. Después de la lluvia toda la ropa de Alfredo es/ está mojada.
15. El abrigo es / está sucio.

16. --¿Cuándo está / es la reunión de estudiantes?

17. Los regalos son / están en la caja roja.

18. De repente, Alfredo es / está tranquilo.

19. Las casas son / están cerca del lago.

20. El toro es / está muerto.

21. Es / está la una y los chicos son / están nerviosos porque del examen.

Solutions to Exercise: Uses of Ser and Estar

Select either ser or estar by underlining the items that follow:

1. Los Angeles es / <u>está</u> en California.

2. --¿Cómo <u>está</u> / es usted hoy, señora Morales?—

--Bien, gracias.--

3. ¿Qué hora <u>es</u> / está?

4. Los estudiantes están / <u>son</u> trabajadores.
5. Las tiendas son / <u>están</u> abiertas durante la noche.
6. La bicicleta <u>es</u>/ está de acero.
7. La fiesta está / <u>es</u> en apartamento de Carolina.

8. --¿De dónde <u>eres</u> / estás tú?--

-- Yo <u>soy</u> / estoy de Guatemala.—
9. Los zapatos están / <u>son</u> de Carlos.
10. Vosotras sois / <u>estáis</u> furiosas porque sale ella.
11. David y yo <u>estamos</u> / somos hablando.
12. Mario <u>es</u> / está abogado y <u>es</u> / está muy serio.
13. Marisol y Beatriz son / <u>están</u> enfermas hoy.

14. Después de la lluvia toda la ropa de Alfredo es/ <u>está</u> mojada.
15. El abrigo es / <u>está</u> sucio.

16. --¿Cuándo está / <u>es</u> la reunión de estudiantes?

17. Los regalos son / <u>están</u> en la caja roja.
18. De repente, Alfredo es / <u>está</u> tranquilo.

19. Las casas son / están cerca del lago.

20. El toro es / está muerto.

21. Es / está la una y los chicos son / están nerviosos porque del examen.

How to Conjugate and Use Irregular Verb *Hacer* in the Present Indicative

Objective: Learn how to conjugate the irregular verb *hacer* in the present indicative.

Method: Memorize *hacer,* say it, write it out.

Outcome: Change *hacer* from its infinitive form to its conjugated form. Use it correctly in exercises that follow.

Singular

1. yo hago = I do, make

2. tú haces = you do, make (familiar)

*3. él/ella hace = he/she/it does, makes

4.usted hace = you do, make (formal)

Plural

†5. nosotros hacemos = we do, make

6. vosotros hacéis = you do, make

+7.ellos/ellas hacen = they do, make

8. ustedes hacen = you do, make

*, †, + *See Appendix A on Page 281 on what these*

symbols mean.

Hacer belongs to a special set of verbs, sometimes called **the *go* verbs**, in which the *yo* portion of the conjugated verb ends in *go*. For example: *yo hago* (*I do, make*). Other frequently used *go* verbs include *tener(tengo), salir(salgo), poner(pongo), decir(digo), venir(vengo), traer(traigo),and oír(oigo)*.

How Hacer Is Used:

1. In its **literal sense** of *to do* or *to make*:
–*Ricardo siempre hace su tarea.* (*Ricardo always does his homework.*).
 –*Los artistas hacen retratos.* (*The artists make portraits.*).

2. In **time expressions** of the type *Hace* + time statement + verb in the present indicative:
–*Hace dos años que Myra vive en San Diego.* (*Myra has been living in San Diego for two years.*).
 –*Hace seis meses que viajo en Bolivia.* (*I have been traveling in Bolivia for six months.*).

3. In **time expressions** of the type: *Verb statement +desde hace* + time statement.
–*Trabajo en la ciudad desde hace diez años.* (*I've been working in the city for 10 years.*).
 –*Ellos cantan en la playa desde hace tres dias.* (*They have been singing on the beach for three days.*).

4. In *expressions related to weather.* The following are frequently used weather expressions formed with *hace*:

–Hace buen tiempo	The weather is good
–Hace mal tiempo	The weather is bad
–Hace frío	It's cold.
–Hace calor	It's hot
–Hace sol	It's sunny
–Hace fresco	It's cool
–Hace viento	It's windy

5. To form the basis for *idiomatic expressions*:

–Hacer cola	To wait in line
–Hacer el papel de	To play the role of
–Hacer las maletas	To pack one's suitcases
–Hacer turismo	To go sightseeing
–Hacer pedazos	To break or tear to pieces
–Hacer una pregunta	To ask a question
–Hacer caso	To mind, pay attention
–Hacer burla de	To make fun of
–Hacer escala	To stop over(plane, boat)
–Hacer clic	To click (with a mouse)

Exercise: Translate Into Spanish Using the Present Indicative of *Hacer*

1. I make bread on Saturday.
2. Paul and Susana make sushi in the kitchen.
3. We do more than the students.
4. He does nothing on Tuesdays.
5. She has been living in Costa Rica for seven years.
6. They have been working here for ten months.
7. My brother and I have been running on the mountain for many years.
8. The weather is good today.
9. When it's sunny we go to the beach.
10. I wear gloves when it's cold.
11. It's windy in spring.
12. It's hot in summer.
13. It's cool in the fall.
14. Anita plays the role of princess in the play.
15. The children pay attention in class.
16. John always asks questions.
17. My family goes sightseeing in September.
18. Perla tears the page to pieces.
19. You all wait in line at Disneyland.
20. I click twice with the mouse.

Solution to Exercise: Translate Into Spanish Using the Present Indicative of *Hacer*

1. Yo hago el pan el sábado.

2. Paul y Susana hacen sushi en la cocina.

3. Nosotros hacemos más que los estudiantes.

4. Él no hace nada los martes.

5. Hace siete años que ella vive en Costa Rica.
6. Hace diez meses que trabajan aqui.
7. Hace muchos años que Mi hermano y yo corremos en la montaña.
8. Hace buen tiempo hoy.
9. Cuando hace sol vamos a la playa.

10. Llevo guantes cuando hace frío.

11. Hace viento en la primavera.
12. Hace calor en el verano.
13. Hace fresco en el otoño.
14. Anita hace el papel de princesa in el drama.
15. Los niños hacen caso en la clase.
16. John siempre hace preguntas.
17. En septiembre mi familia hace turismo.

18. Perla hace pedazos de la página.

19. Ustedes hacen cola en Disneyland.

20. Hago clic dos veces con el ratón.

How to Conjugate and Use the Verb *Tener* in the Present Indicative

Objective: Learn how to conjugate the irregular verb *tener* in the present indicative.
Method: Memorize *tener,* say it, write it out.
Outcome: Change *tener* from its infinitive form to its conjugated form. Use it correctly in exercises that follow.

Below is the verb *tener* (to have) in its conjugated form:
Singular
1. yo tengo = I have

2. tú tienes = you have (familiar)

3. él/ella tiene = he/she/it has

4. usted tiene = you have (formal)
Plural
5. nosotros/as tenemos = we have

6. vosotros/as tenéis = you have (Spain)

7. ellos/ellas tienen = they have
8. ustedes tienen = you all have

How Tener Is Used

Tener is used in 3 basic contexts:

1. In it's literal meaning of *to have, to hold*, or *to possess*. For example
- *El estudiante tiene tres libros*. (The student has 3 books).
- *Ustedes no tienen el carro azul*. (You don't have the blue   car).
2. When *tener* is paired with *que*. **Tener que** express a strong obligation or desire to do something, best rendered by the English translation "must". For example
- *Yo tengo que estudiar para mis examenes el lunes*. (I must study for my exams on Monday).
- *Miguel tiene que salir en seguida*. (Miguel must leave   at once).

3. *Tener* is often used in common idiomatic expressions. Although *tener* means *to have* or *to hold*, it also has an idiomatic meaning of *to be*, or *to feel*.
For example
- *Mario tiene sed porque no hay agua*. (Mario is thirsty because there is no water).
- *Paula y yo tenemos ganas de comer tacos hoy*. (Paula and I feel like eating tacos today).

Here is a partial list of idiomatic expressions using *tener*.

Tener hambre = to be hungry
Tener sed = to be thirsty
Tener sueño = to be sleepy

Tener razón = to be right
Tener suerte = to be lucky
Tener calma = to be calm
Tener éxito = to be successful
Tener calor = to be hot
Tener frío = to be cold
Tener cuidado = to be careful
Tener miedo = to be afraid
Tener miedo de = to be afraid of
Tener prisa = to be in a hurry
Tener vergüenza = to be ashamed
Tener (number) años = to be (number) years old.
Tener ganas de + infinitive = to feel like

Note: Never use *tener* to form a perfect tense as in: She has gone to New York. Use the verb haber instead. *Ella ha ido a Nueva York.*

Exercise: Conjugate Tener

1. <u>Las chicas </u>(tener) _____ dos mochilas.
2. <u>Yo</u> no (tener) _____ comida.
3. <u>Ustedes </u>(tener) _____ la blusa morada.
4. <u>Miguel y yo</u> (tener) _____ muchos amigos.
5. <u>Pilar</u> no (tener) _____ sueño.
6. <u>Mi hermano</u> (tener) mucho hambre.
7. <u>Tú</u> no (tener) _____ ganas de trabajar.
8. <u>Maribel </u>(tener) _____ frío hoy.
9. <u>El pájaro </u>(tener) _____ un nido en el árbol.
10. <u>Graciela</u> (tener) _____ tamales deliciosos.
11. <u>Abuelita y mi tío</u> no (tener) _____ el diccionario.
12. <u>Su compañero </u>(tener) _____ una casa grande.
13. <u>Perla</u> (tener) _____ suerte en Las Vegas.
14. <u>Mis padres </u>(tener) _____ dos hijas y tres hijos.
15. <u>Ella</u> (tener) una camiseta amarilla.
16. <u>María</u> y sus hermanos nunca (tener) _____ su tarea.
17. <u>El salón de clase</u> no (tener) _____ bastante sillas.
18. <u>Ustedes</u> no (tener) _____ éxito.
19. <u>Ellos</u> (tener) _____ patines verdes.
20. <u>Mi amigo y yo</u> (tener) _____ el libro de español.

Solutions to Exercise: Conjugate Tener

1. Las chicas (tener) tienen dos mochilas.
2. Yo no (tener) tengo comida.
3. Ustedes (tener) tienen la blusa morada.
4. Miguel y yo (tener) tenemos muchos amigos.
5. Pilar no (tener) tiene sueño.
6. Mi hermano (tener) tiene mucho hambre.
7. Tú no (tener) tienes ganas de trabajar.
8. Maribel (tener) tiene frío hoy.
9. El pájaro (tener) tiene un nido en el árbol.
10. Graciela (tener) tiene tamales deliciosos.
11. Abuelita y mi tío no (tener) tienen el diccionario.
12. Su compañero (tener) tiene una casa grande.
13. Perla (tener) tiene suerte en Las Vegas.
14. Mis padres (tener) tienen dos hijas y tres hijos.
15. Ella (tener) tiene una camiseta amarilla.
16. María y sus hermanos nunca (tener) tienen su tarea.
17. El salón de clase no (tener) tiene bastante sillas.
18. Ustedes no (tener) tienen éxito.
19. Ellos (tener) tienen patines verdes.
20. Mi amigo y yo (tener) tenemos el libro de español.

Exercise: Write 10 Sentences Using Idiomatic Expressions Formed with *Tener*

Select any ten of the idiomatic expressions in this lesson – *tener hambre*, *tener sed* etc. and use each of them to write a sentence, ten total. Five of your sentences must start with singular subjects (ex. Yo, or mi amigo). The remaining five must start with plural subjects (ex. nosotros, or Marcos y Ana). Translate each of your Spanish sentences into English.

Solutions to Exercise: Write 10 Sentences Using Idiomatic Expressions Formed with *Tener*

Answers will vary. Here are some possibilities for five:

1. Miguel tiene sueño despues de trabajar.

2. Tienes razón. Dos más dos son cuatro.

3. Los bebitos tienen calma en el carro.
4. Siempre tengo éxito cuando practico mucho.
5. Nosotros tenemos frío en el invierno.

Ir: Present Indicative Tense

Objective: Learn how to conjugate the irregular verb *ir* in the present indicative.
Method: Memorize *ir,* say it, write it out.
Outcome: Change *ir* from its infinitive form to its conjugated form. Use it correctly in exercises that follow.

Singular
1. yo voy = I go

2. tú vas = you go (familiar)

3. el/ella va = he/she/it goes
4. usted va = you go (formal)

Plural
5. nosotros vamos = we go
6. vosotros vais = you go
7. ellos/ellas van = they go
8. ustedes van = you go

Exercise: Match the underlined items with the correct form of *ir* in the present tense

Example: <u>Ella</u> ir *a* la fiesta. → <u>Ella</u> *va a* la fiesta.

1. <u>Ellos</u> no ir.
2. <u>Tú</u> ir para la escuela.
3. <u>Miguel</u> ir con sus amigos.
4. <u>Yo</u> no ir hoy.
5. <u>Ariel y yo</u> ir a las seis.
6. <u>Usted</u> ir al parque.
7. <u>Los chicos</u> ir a La Jolla.
8. <u>Los pajaros</u> ir a sus nidos.
9. <u>Nosotros</u> ir a San Clemente.
10. <u>Ustedes</u> no ir a la biblioteca.
11. <u>Sus abuelos</u> ir en el verano.
12. <u>Perla y tu</u> ir a Las Vegas.
13. <u>Mi papá</u> no ir los sábados.
14. <u>Nosotros</u> no ir en el gimnasio.
15. <u>María</u> nunca ir a Tijuana.
16. <u>Los estudiantes</u> no ir en la clase de historia.
17. <u>Mi tía</u> ir a la tienda.
18. <u>Javier</u> ir de compras.
19. <u>La familia Garcia</u> ir al concierto.
20. <u>Yo</u> no ir a mi cuarto.

Solution to Exercise: Match the underlined items with the correct form of *ir* in the present tense

Example: <u>Ella</u> ir *a* la fiesta. → <u>Ella</u> *va a* la fiesta.

1. <u>Ellos</u> no van.
2. <u>Tú</u> vas para la escuela.
3. <u>Miguel</u> va con sus amigos.
4. <u>Yo</u> no voy hoy.
5. <u>Ariel y yo</u> vamos a las seis.
6. <u>Usted</u> va al parque.
7. <u>Los chicos</u> van a La Jolla.
8. <u>Los pájaros</u> van a sus nidos.
9. <u>Nosotros</u> vamos a San Clemente.
10. <u>Ustedes</u> no van a la biblioteca.
11. <u>Sus abuelos</u> van en el verano.
12. <u>Perla y tu</u> van a Las Vegas.
13. <u>Mi papá</u> no va los sábados.
14. <u>Nosotros</u> no vamos en el gimnasio.
15. <u>María</u> nunca va a Tijuana.
16. <u>Los estudiantes</u> no van en la clase de historia.
17. <u>Mi tía</u> va a la tienda.
18. <u>Javier</u> va de compras.
19. <u>La familia Garcia</u> va al concierto.
20. <u>Yo</u> no voy a mi cuarto.

Four Steps in Using Ir + a + the Infinitive To talk about the Future

Objective: Learn how to use *ir* and the infinitive to talk about the future.

Method: Outline the 4-step process of combining *ir* and the infinitive to speak and write about the future.

Outcome: Demonstrate mastery by correctly performing exercises that follow.

Using Ir to Talk about the Future in 4 Steps

Step 1: Conjugate the verb **ir** (to go) in the present indicative as is done below, for example, ***yo voy***.

Singular
1. yo voy = I go

2. tú vas = you go (familiar)

3. el/ella va = he/she/it goes
4. usted va = you go (formal)

Plural
5. nosotros vamos = we go
6. vosotros vais = you go
7. ellos/ellas van = they go
8. ustedes van = you go

Step 2: Add ***a*** and an infinitive of your choice. For example, *hablar*.

Step 3: Add a few words after the infinitive, if necessary, so the sentence has more meaning. For example, *con Miguel*.

Step 4: Put Steps 1, 2, 3, and 4 together to get, *Yo voy a hablar con Miguel*. (I am going to speak with Miguel, or I will speak with Miguel, or I plan to speak with Miguel.)

Exercise: Ir + a + the Infinitive

Follow steps 1 through 4 to write sentences using the infinitives 1-20 below and their add-ons. Make sure you use all 8 items in the conjugated verb *ir*.

Model: acampar en el parque.

      Nosotros vamos a acampar en el parque.

1. beber un vaso de agua.
2. comer los tacos.
3. esperar mi amiga.
4. estudiar en la biblioteca.
5. vivir en Nueva York.
6. bailar en la fiesta.
7. salir para la escuela.
8. alquilar un apartamento.
9. reparar el carro.
10. visitor a Los Angeles.
11. correr por la playa.
12. escribir cartas.
13. mirar los libros.
14. hacer la tarea.
15. ver la tele.

16. jugar al fútbol.
17. preparar la comida.
18. trabajar en McDonalds.
19. ir de compras.
20. montar en bicicleta.

Solutions to Exercise: Ir + a + the Infinitive

Answers will vary. Here are examples of some possibilities for the first 5 items:

1. Ellos van a beber un vaso de agua
2. Adam va a comer los tacos.
3. Nosotros vamos a esperar mi amiga.
4. Ustedes van a estudar en la biblioteca.

5. Tú no vas a vivir en Nueva York.

Part 3

Gustar, Stem-changing Verbs in the Present Indicative

Gustar: Stating preferences and Discussing Activities

How to Conjugate and Use *Gustar* in the Present Indicative

Objective: Learn how to conjugate and use *gustar* in the present indicative.

Method: Combine *gustar* (to like) and the infinitive to show like, dislike, or preference for an activity.

Outcome: Demonstrate mastery of *gustar* by correctly performing exercises that follow.

Singular
1. Me gusta = I like
2. Le gusta = you (fam.) like
3. Le gusta = he/she/it likes
4. Le gusta = you (form.) like

Plural
5. Nos gusta = we like
6. Os gusta = you like
7. Les gusta = they like
8. Les gusta = you like

A word for word translation of *me gusta* to English is: *to me it is pleasing*. Spanish does not have a direct equivalent of *I like, you like* etc. The

English translations you see in the conjugation above, are approximate only. *Me, te, le, nos, os, les* are **all indirect object pronouns** and, for now, all you have to remember is:

(a) when it is conjugated, *gustar* takes the indirect object pronouns.

(b) The following are the English meanings of the Spanish indirect object pronouns:

Singular
1. me = to me
2. te = to you (fam)
3. le = to him/her/it
4. le = to you (formal)

Plural
5. nos = to us
6. os = to you (Spain only)
7. les = to them
8. les = to you

How to use Gustar with Singular Nouns

1. Use *el* in front of a masculine noun:
−*Me gusta el helado.* (*I like ice cream.*).
−*Les gusta el pastel.* (*They like cake.*)
   Use *la* in front of a feminine noun:
−*Me gusta la leche.* (*I like milk.*).
−*Nos gusta la television.* (*We like television.*)

How to use Gustar with Plural Nouns

2. If you like **more than one thing**, then **gusta becomes gustan**:

–*Me gusta el libro.* (*I like the book.*) → *Me gustan los libros.* (*I like the books.*)

–*Les gusta el pastel.* (*They like the cake.*) → *Les gustan los pasteles.* (*They like the cakes.*)

How to use *gustar* with names:

Gustar with one name:

3. Use **a** in front of the name and **le** after it **followed by *gusta***:

–*A Maribel **le gusta** comer.* (*Maribel likes to eat.*).

–*A* Patricio **le** *gusta la música.* (*Patricio likes music.*)

Gustar with two or more names:

1. Use **a** in front of each name and **les** after it **followed by *gusta***:

–*A Maribel y a Pablo **les gusta** comer.* (*Maribel and Pablo like to eat.*).

–*A* Patricio y *a* su hermano **les gusta** *la música.* (*Patricio and his brother like music.*)

How to Be more Precise when Using Gustar with Le and Les

4. In a statement such as *Le gusta la comida*, it's sometimes difficult to know if the *le* refers to him, her, it, or you. Here's what to do:

<u>Singular</u>

If it's **him**, use *a él* –*A él le gusta la comida.*(He likes the food).
If it's **her**, use *a ella* – *A ella le gusta la comida.* (She likes the food).

If it's **you** (formal), use *a usted* –*A usted le gusta correr.*(You like to run).
If it's **an animal**, use *a* with the type of animal – *Al perro le gusta la comida.* (The (male)dog likes the food).
A la perra le gusta la comida. (The (female) dog likes the food).

<u>Plural</u>
In a statement such as *Les gusta la comida*, we have the same problem. Here's what to do:

If it's **them**, use *a ellos/as* –A ellos les gusta el carro. (They (masculine)like the car).

–A ellas les gusta el carro. (They (feminine) like the car).

If it's **you**, use *a ustedes* – *A ustedes les gusta el carro.* (you (all) like the car).

If *them* refers to animals use *a* with the type of animal – *A los perros les gusta la juguete.* (The (male)dogs like the toy).

91

–A las perras les gusta la juguete. (The (female) dogs like the toy).

How to Say No or Not with Gustar

5. Always place **no** in front of the words: **me, te le, nos, os, les** and **nowhere else** in sentences with *gustar.*
–No me gusta la historia. (*I don't like history.*)

–No te gusta el té. (*You don't like tea.*)

How to Add Emphasis with Gustar

6. In order to say a person or thing ***really likes something***, or likes doing something, add the following to the conjugated forms of gustar:
Singular

1. **A mí** me gusta = I (*really*) like

2. **A ti** te gusta = you (*really*) (fam.) like

3. **A él**, **a ella** le gusta = he/she/it (*really*) likes

4. **A usted** le gusta = you (form.) (*really*) like
Plural
5. **A nosotros/as** nos gusta = we (*really*) like
6. **A vosotros/as** os gusta = you (*really*) like
7. **A ellos/as** les gusta = they (*really*) like
8. **A ustedes** les gusta = you (*really*) like

For example:

–*A ella le gusta ir de compras*. (She really likes shopping).
–*A ustedes les gusta jugar al tenis*. (You really like playing tennis).

How to Form Questions with Gustar

7. Normally the only distinction between a statement and a question when using *gustar* is a question mark when writing or a rise in voice pitch at the end of the sentence when speaking.
Statement –*Le gusta el flan. (He likes the flan.)*
Question –*¿Le gusta el flan? (Does he like the flan?)*
When there is a **question** with the name of a person, the **name comes after the expression with gustar**.
Statement –*A Jorge le gusta el flan. (Jorge likes the flan.)*
Question –*¿Le gusta el flan **a Jorge**? (Does Jorge like the flan?)*

Other verbs that follow the same conjugated pattern of *Gustar* are: *doler,(to hurt), faltar(to need), quedar(to have, remain), encantar(to really like),* and *fascinar (to fascinate)*

Exercise: How to Use Gustar in the Present Indicative

With singular nouns
1. She likes the car.
2. They like the book.
3. We like the pen

With plural nouns
4. He likes the apples.
5. You all like the beaches.
6. I like the oranges.

With singular names
7. John likes old cars.

8. Alán likes the bicycle

9. Mary likes the shirt.

With plural names/nouns
10. Pamela and Vincente like the ice cream.
11. The dogs like meat.
12. Paco, Ken, and Raul like to play baseball.

Negating
13. I do not like to run.
14. Anita does not like to draw.
15. We do not like to study.

Adding emphasis
16. You (fam.) really like to go shopping.
17. We really like to surf.
18. I really like to watch television.

Adding precision when using le and les
19. She likes to eat tacos.
20. You (formal) do not like to do homework.

21.   He likes to play soccer.

Forming questions that involve someone's name

22.   Does Maribel like the house?
23.   Do Sofia and Miguel like the photo?
24.   Does Jonathan like the blue shirt?

Solutions to Exercise: How to Use Gustar in the Present Indicative

With singular nouns
1.   Le gusta el carro.
2.   Les gusta el libro.
3.   Nos gusta la pluma.

With plural nouns
4.   Le gustan las manzanas.
5.   Les gustan las playas.
6.   Me gustan las naranjas.

With singular names
7.   A John les gustan los carros viejos.

8.   A Alán le gusta la bicicleta.

9.   A Mary le gusta la camisa.

With plural names/nouns
10.   A Pamela y a Vincente les gusta el helado.
11.   A los perros les gusta la carne.
12.   A Paco, a Ken, y a Raul les gusta jugar

        béisbol.

Negating
13.   No me gusta correr
14.   A Anita no le gusta dibujar.
15.   No nos gusta estudiar.

Adding emphasis
16.   A ti te gusta ir de compras.
17.   A nosotros nos gusta surfear.

18.   A mí me gusta mirar la televisión.

Adding precision when using le and les

19.   A ella le gusta comer tacos.

20.   A usted no le gusta hacer la tarea.

21.   A él le gusta jugar fútbol.

Forming questions that involve someone's name

22.   ¿Le gusta la casa a Maribel?

23.   ¿Les gusta la foto a Sofia y a Miguel?

24.   ¿Le gusta la camisa azul a Jonathan?

Activities Bank to Use with Gustar

Here is a list of activities you may use with the verb gustar:

Beber.   To drink.

Comer.   To eat.

Correr.   To run.

Cuidar a mi hermanito/a. To take care of my little brother/sister.

Comunicar por Facebook.
                        To keep in touch on Facebook.

Descansar.   To rest.

Escuchar musica.   to listen to music.

Escribir correos electronicos.
                        To write emails.

Estudiar.   To study.

Hacer la tarea.   To do homework.

Ir a la iglesia.   To go to church.

Ir a la playa.   To go to the beach.

Ir al gimnasio.   To go to the gym

Ir al restaurante.   To go to a restaurant.

Ir de compras.   To go shopping.

Preparar la comida.   To prepare a meal.

Andar en patineta.   To skateboard.

Practicar deportes.   To play sports.

Hablar por telefono con...To talk on the phone with...

Jugar juegos de video. To play video games.

Jugar al baloncesto.   To play basketball.

Jugar al fútbol americano.   To play football.

Jugar al fútbol.   To play soccer.

Jugar al béisbol.   To play baseball.

Leer un libro.   To read a book.

Nadar.   To swim.

Montar en bicicleta.   To ride a bicycle.

Mirar la televisión. To watch TV.

Pasear.   To go for a walk.

Pasar un rato con los amigos.
            To spend time with friends.
Sacar la basura.   To take out the trash.
Sacar al perro.   To take the dog for a walk.
Surfear.   To surf.
Tocar el piano/la guitarra/la flauta etc.
To play the piano/guitar/flute etc.
Viajar con mi familia.   To travel with my family.

Stem-Changing Verbs: Present Indicative

Objective: Learn how to form the 4 types of stem-changing verbs in the present indicative.

Method: Explain or outline where and how stem vowels change in the 4 types of stem-changing verbs.

Outcome: Demonstrate mastery by correctly completing exercises that follow on stem-changing verbs.

Important Terms

Infinitive form: Spanish verbs are in their infinitive form when they end with **ar**, or **er**, or **ir**. These endings are called infinitive endings. For example, **comenzar**, **querer**, **preferir**.

Stem: The stem of a verb is what remains when you drop its infinitive ending. For example, the stem of **comenzar** is **comenz**, the stem of **querer** is **quer**, and the stem of **preferir** is **prefer**.

The **stem vowel**: The vowel that changes in the stem when the verb is conjugated. The stem vowels in the following verbs are bolded and underlined: com**e**nzar, qu**e**rer, pref**e**rir. In the present indicative, there are four types of stem vowel changes.

Type 1: Among verbs whose stem vowels change from e to ie (e>ie) is *querer* (to wish, to love, to want). Note that this vowel change takes place when the verb is conjugated, as it is below, in all but the nosotros and vosotros portions of the verb.

<u>Singular</u>
1. yo quiero = I wish

2. tú quieres = you (fam.) wish

3. él/ella quiere = he/she/it wishes

4. usted quiere = you (form.) wish
<u>Plural</u>
5. nosotros queremos = we wish

6. vosotros queréis = you wish

7. ellos/ellas quieren = they wish
8. ustedes quieren = you wish

Other verbs that undergo the e>ie change are:

-ar	-er	-ir
comenzar	defender	mentir
empezar	encender	preferir
negar	entender	
pensar		

Type 2: Among verbs whose stem vowels change from o to ue (o>ue) is *contar* (to count). Note that this vowel change takes place in all except the nosotros and vosotros portions of the verb.

<u>Singular</u>

1. yo cuento = I count

2. tú cuentas = you (fam.) count

3. él/ella cuenta = he/she/it counts

 4. usted cuenta = you (form.) count

<u>Plural</u>

5. nosotros contamos = we count

6. vosotros contáis = you count

7. ellos/ellas cuentan = they count
8. ustedes cuentan = you count

Other verbs that undergo the o>ue change are:

-ar	-er	-ir
costar	devolver	morir
encontrar	llover	dormir
recordar	mover	
probar	poder	

Type 3: Among verbs whose stem vowels change from e to i (e>i) is *pedir* (to ask for). Note that this vowel change takes place when the verb is conjugated, as it is below, in all but the nosotros and vosotros portions of the verb.

<u>Singular</u>
1. yo pido = I ask for

2. tú pides = you (fam.) ask for

3. él/ella pide = he/she/it asks for
4. usted pide = you (form.) ask for

<u>Plural</u>
5. nosotros pedimos = we ask for

6. vosotros pedís = you ask for

7. ellos/ellas piden = they ask for
8. ustedes piden = you ask for

Other verbs that undergo the e>ie change are:

competir	medir	seguir
corregir	reír	servir
despedir	repetir	vestir
elegir	seguir	

Type 4: *Jugar* (to play) is the only verb in Spanish whose stem vowel changes from u to ue (u>ue). Note that this vowel change takes place in all except the nosotros and vosotros portions of the verb.

<u>Singular</u>
1. yo juego = I play

2. tú juegas = you play (familiar)

3. él/ella juega = he/she/it plays

4. usted juega = you play (formal)

<u>Plural</u>
5. nosotros jugamos = we play

6. vosotros jugáis = you play

7. ellos/ellas juegan = they play
8. ustedes juegan = you play

Exercise: Stem-Changing Verbs Part A

1. Select 1verb from each of the stem-changing verb types 1, 2, 3, and 4.
2. Conjugate each of your verbs so that they appear in the side by side format as represented by the verb *jugar* in the example below.

Singular   Plural

1. yo juego = I play   5. nosotros jugamos = we play

2. tú juegas = you (fam.) play   6. vosotros jugáis = you play

3. él/ella juega = he/she/it plays   7. ellos/ellas juegan = they play

4. usted juega = you (form.) play   8. ustedes juegan = you play

3. Draw a single shape in which you <u>enclose</u> those parts of the verb whose stem vowels change. In this way those parts of the verb where the stem vowel remains unchanged will be on the outside of the shape you draw.
4. Does the shape you drew remind you of an everyday object? If so what is it?
5 Based on the shape you drew you might say that stem-changing verbs might also be called _____ verbs.

Solution to Exercise: Stem-Changing Verbs Part A

<u>Singular</u>   <u>Plural</u>

1. yo juego = I play   5. nosotros jugamos = we play

2. tú juegas = you (fam.) play   6. vosotros jugáis = you play

3. él/ella juega = he/she/it plays   7. ellos/ellas juegan = they play
4. usted juega = you (form.) play   8. ustedes juegan = you play

The shape should remind you of a shoe or something close to it.

Based on the shape you drew, you might say that stem-changing verbs might also be called **<u>shoe</u>** verbs. In fact, stem-changing verbs are often called *shoe* verbs for this reason.

Exercise: Stem-Changing Verbs Part B

Match the underlined pronouns and nouns with the correct conjugated form of the verb in parentheses.

Stem-changing verbs, Type 1(e>ie)

1. <u>Yo</u> (preferir) _____los zapatos rojos.

2. <u>Los maestros</u> (pensar) _____que los estudiantes son inteligentes.

3. <u>Mi hermano y yo</u> (encender) _____ la luz.

4. <u>Lina</u> no (entender) _____el francés.

5. <u>Nosotros</u> (defender) _____los derechos humanos.

Stem-changing verbs, Type 2 (o>ue)

6. <u>Manolo y Joaquin</u> (contar) _____el dinero.

7. <u>Nosotros</u> (poder) _____ estudiar en el parque.

8. <u>La Señora Chavez</u> (mover) _____su hijo al otro lado de la calle.

9. <u>Ellos</u> (probar) _____el helado antes de comprarlo.

10. <u>Carlito</u> no (encontrar) _____con nadie.

11. <u>El niño y yo</u> (devolver) _____la fruta.

Stem-changing verbs, Type 3(e>i)

12. <u>La gente</u> (elegir) _____ el presidente.

13. <u>Él</u> que (reír) _____ más vive mejor.

14. <u>Los chicos</u> nos (pedir) _____ dinero.

15. <u>El carro</u> no (servir) _____ para nada.

16. <u>Vosotras</u> no (repetir) _____ las palabras.

Stem-changing verbs, Type 4 (u>ue)

17. <u>Yo</u> (jugar) _____ al tenis hoy.

18. <u>Pedro</u> nunca (jugar) _____ al béisbol.

19. <u>Carla y yo</u> (jugar) _____ con la pelota.

20. <u>Ellos</u> (jugar) _____ los lunes y los jueves.

21. <u>El equipo</u> (jugar) _____ mañana.

Solutions to Exercise: Stem-Changing Verbs
Part B

Match the underlined pronouns and nouns with the correct conjugated form of the verb in parentheses.

Stem-changing verbs, Type 1(e>ie)
1. <u>Yo</u> (preferir) <u>prefiero</u> los zapatos rojos.
2. <u>Los maestros</u> (pensar) <u>piensan</u> que los estudiantes son inteligentes.
3. <u>Mi hermano y yo</u> (encender) <u>encendemos</u> la luz.
4. <u>Lina</u> no (entender) <u>entiende</u> el francés.
5. <u>Nosotros</u> (defender) <u>defendemos</u> los derechos humanos.

Stem-changing verbs, Type 2(o>ue)
6. <u>Manolo y Joaquin</u> (contar) <u>cuentan</u> el dinero.
7. <u>Nosotros</u> (poder) <u>podemos</u> estudiar en el parque.
8. <u>La Señora Chavez</u> (mover) <u>mueve</u> su hijo al otro lado de la calle.
9. <u>Ellos</u> (probar) <u>prueban</u> el helado antes de comprarlo.
10. <u>Carlito</u> no (encontrar) <u>encuentra</u> con   nadie.
11. <u>El niño y yo</u> (devolver) <u>devolvemos</u> la fruta.

Stem-changing verbs, Type 3 (e>i)

12.   La gente (elegir) elige el presidente.

13.   Él que (reír) ríe más vive mejor.

14.   Los chicos nos (pedir) piden dinero.

15.   El carro no (servir) sirve para nada.

16.   Vosotras no (repetir) repetís las palabras.

Stem-changing verb, Type 4 (u>ue)

17.   Yo (jugar) juego al tenis hoy.

18.   Pedro nunca (jugar) juega al béisbol.

19.   Carla y yo (jugar) jugamos con la pelota.

20.   Ellos (jugar) juegan los lunes y los jueves.

21.   El equipo (jugar) juega mañana.

Exercise: Stem-Changing Verbs Types 1 Through 4, Blended

1. <u>Ella</u> (dormir) _____ en su cuarto.
2. <u>Los cazadores</u> (seguir) _____ el venado.
3. <u>Ellos</u> (jugar) _____ para el campeonato mundial.
4. <u>Johanna</u> nunca (mentir) _____.
5. <u>Liset y Mariana</u> (vestir) _____ a su hermano menor.
6. <u>Sofia y yo</u> (encontrar) _____ el libro viejo.
7. ¿(Jugar) _____ <u>vosotros</u> al fútbol?
8. <u>Los ninos</u> (repetir) _____ las letras del alfabeto.
9. <u>Ustedes</u> (pensar) _____ en la pizza y Coca Cola.
10. <u>La pluma</u> (costar) _____ muy cara.
11. <u>Nosotros</u> (jugar) _____ una partida el domingo.
12. <u>Los cantantes</u> (competir) _____para el título de campeón hoy.
13. <u>El año nuevo</u> (empezar) _____el jueves.
14. ¿(Recordar) _____ <u>ustedes</u> lo qué hacemos?
15. <u>Paula y Marta</u> (preferir) _____

quedarse en casa.

16.   Yo (negar) _____ que ella tiene el carro hoy.

17.   --Juanito ¿ Por qué (jugar) _____ tú con el fuego?--

18.   Él no (poder) _____nadar mucho.

19.   Vosotros siempre (jugar) _____en la playa.

20.   Susanna (medir) _____la planta con la cinta métrica.

Solutions to Exercise: Stem-Changing Verbs
Types 1 Through 4, Blended

1.   <u>Ella</u> (dormir) <u>duerme</u> en su cuarto.
2.   <u>Los cazadores</u> (seguir) <u>siguen</u> el venado.
3.   <u>Ellos</u> (jugar) <u>juegan</u> para el campeonato mundial.
4.   <u>Johanna</u> nunca (mentir) <u>miente</u>.
5.   <u>Liset y Mariana</u> (vestir) <u>visten</u> a su hermano menor.
6.   <u>Sofia y yo</u> (encontrar) <u>encontramos</u> el libro viejo.
7.   ¿(Jugar) <u>jugáis</u>   vosotros al fútbol?
8.   <u>Los ninos</u> (repetir) <u>repiten</u> las letras del alfabeto.
9.   <u>Ustedes</u> (pensar) <u>piensan</u> en la pizza y Coca Cola.
10.   <u>La pluma</u> (costar) <u>cuesta</u> muy cara .
11.   <u>Nosotros</u> (jugar) <u>jugamos</u> una partida el domingo.
12.   <u>Los cantantes</u> (competir) <u>compiten</u> para el título de campeón hoy.
13.   <u>El año nuevo</u> (empezar) <u>empieza</u> el jueves.
14.   ¿(Recordar) <u>recuerden</u> ustedes lo qué hacemos?

15. <u>Paula y Marta</u> (preferir) <u>prefieren</u> quedarse en casa.

16. <u>Yo</u> (negar) <u>niego</u> que ella tiene el carro hoy.

17. --Juanito ¿ Por qué (jugar) <u>juegas</u> <u>tú</u> con el fuego?--

18. <u>Él</u> no (poder) <u>puede</u> nadar mucho.

19. <u>Vosotros</u> siempre (jugar) <u>jugáis</u> en la playa.

20. <u>Susanna</u> (medir) <u>mide</u> la planta con la cinta métrica.

Part 4

The Past Tenses

The Past Tenses

There are two simple past tenses in the Spanish indicative. They are the ***Preterite*** and the ***Imperfect***. They are known as simple past tenses to differentiate them from the compound tenses that have a helping (or auxiliary) verb such as *have*. Although they are both used to represent past action, they are used differently.

The Preterite

Objective: Learn how to conjugate and use regular verbs in the preterite.

Method: Memorize a model *-ar, -er,* and *-ir* verb in the preterite tense.

Outcome: Explain how to change any regular *-ar, -er,* and *-ir* verb from its infinitive form to its conjugated preterite form. Correctly complete the exercises that follow.

How the Preterite Is Used

    a. to tell of an event that was limited in time by words or phrases indicating how long, number of times, or when.

    Example *–Ayer hablé por teléfono con mi amigo.* (Yesterday I spoke by telephone with my friend).

    –La semana pasada salimos con María dos veces. (Last week we went out with Maria two times).

    b. To relate a series of past actions. Example

    –Habló con su papá, subió al autobús, y

    salió. (He spoke to his father, boarded the bus, and left).

    c. To indicate a change in emotional or physical state after a triggering event.

–Estuvimos furiosos cuando Mario ganó el premio tres veces. (We were (became) furious when Mario won the prize three times).

Preterite Formation Regular Verbs

There are 2 basic steps in conjugating a regular *-ar* verb such as *tomar* (to take, to drink) in the preterite:

1. Drop the infinitive ending of *tomar* and keep the stem *tom.*
2. Add the preterite endings for *ar* verbs:

Singular: **é**, *aste*, **ó**, **ó**

Plural: *amos*, *asteis*, *aron*, *aron*
that matches what you wish to say or write.

Singular

1. yo tom**é** = I drank

2. tú tom**aste** = you (fam.) drank

3. él/ella tom**ó** = he/she/it drank

4. usted tom**ó** = you (form.) drank

Plural

5. nosotros tom**amos** = we drank

6. vosotros tom**asteis** = you drank

7. ellos/ellas tom**aron** = they drank.

8. ustedes tom**aron** = you drank

There are 2 basic steps in conjugating a regular *-er* or *-ir* verb in the preterite. Note that the endings for both *-er* and *-ir* verbs are the same.

1. Drop the infinitive ending of *comer* or

vivir and keep the stem *com* or *viv*.
2. Add the preterite endings for- *er or -ir*

verbs: Singular: *í, iste, ió, ió*

Plural: *imos, isteis, ieron, ieron*
that matches what you wish to say or write.

Singular   ## Plural

1. yo comí = I ate   5. nosotros com**imos** = we ate

2. tú com**iste** = you (fam.) ate   6. vosotros com**isteis** = you eat

3. él/ella com**ío** = he/she/it ate   7.ellos/ellas com**ieron** = they ate.

4. usted com**ío** = you (form.) ate   8. ustedes com**ieron** = you ate

Singular   ## Plural

1. yo viví = I lived   5. nosotros viv**imos** = we lived

2. tú viv**iste** = you (fam.) lived   6. vosotros viv**isteis** = you lived

3. él/ella viv**ío** = he/she/it lived   7.ellos/ellas viv**ieron** = they lived

4.usted viv**ío** = you (form.) lived   8. ustedes viv**ieron** = you lived

Some verbs undergo spelling changes. Verbs
ending in *–car (bus**car**)*, *–gar (pa**gar**)*, and *–zar
(comen**zar**)* are the only ones that will be dealt
with here. There are other spelling changes but
these will be left for the second year of Spanish.
These verbs change in the **yo form only**. The rest
is conjugated normally:

Buscar (to look for) *-car*→**qué**
Singular

yo busqué = I looked for
tú buscaste = you (familiar) looked for
él/ella buscó = he/she/it looked for
usted buscó = you (formal) looked for
Plural
nosotros/as buscamos = we looked for
vosotros/as buscasteis = you (Spain) looked for
ellos/as buscaron = they looked for
ustedes buscaron = you looked for

Other verbs like *buscar* are : *aplicar, chocar, explicar, secar, marcar, masticar, platicar, sacar, tocar, publicar*.

Pagar (to pay) -*gar*→**gué**

Singular
yo pagué = I paid
tú pagaste = you (familiar) paid
él/ella pagó = he/she/it paid
usted pagó = you (formal) paid

Plural
nosotros/as pagamos = we paid
vosotros/as pagasteis = you (Spain) paid
ellos/as pagaron = they paid
ustedes pagaron = you paid

Other verbs like *pagar* are : *apagar, colgar, fregar, llegar, pegar, jugar, negar*.

Comenzar (to begin, start) *-zar*→**cé**
Singular
yo comencé = I began
tú comenzaste = you (familiar) began
él/ella comenzó = he/she/it began
usted comenzó = you (formal) paid
Plural
nosotros/as comenzamos = we began
vosotros/as comenzasteis = you (Spain) began
ellos/as comenzaron = they began
ustedes comenzaron = you began

Other verbs like *comenzar* are : *almorzar, alzar, avanzar, cruzar, rechazar, utilizar*.

Exercise: The Preterite, Regular Verbs

Rewrite each sentence so that the underlined verb in the infinitive is changed into its correct preterite form.

1. Juan y yo <u>hablar</u> por teléfono con papá.

2. Ustedes <u>mirar</u> las flores el sábado pasado.

3. Anoche mis nietas me <u>escribir</u> un correo electrónico.

4. Usted <u>tomar</u> el autobus a las seis de la tarde.

5. Mark nunca <u>pelear</u> el jueves pasado.

6. Su sobrino <u>trabajar</u> en la tienda por un mes.

7. Los médicos <u>entrar</u> a decirnos que era tiempo de salir.

8. Ellas me <u>abrazar</u> e inmediatamente yo sentía una ola de calma.

9. Tú <u>abrir</u> los ojos a las doce en punto.

10. El gato <u>llegar</u> el año pasado

11. La princesa <u>ofrecer</u> una recompensa a

los políticos.

12. Los duques valientes <u>rechazar</u> el rey en 1544.

13. Ella <u>contestar</u> tres preguntas.

14. Las enfermeras <u>llegar</u> y le hicieron la prueba del alcohol.

15. Miguel <u>terminar</u> el viaje en enero.

16. Cuando Daniel y David <u>salir</u> del salón de clase, no habían hecho la tarea.

17. Mi novia <u>comprar</u> un anillo de oro para mi.

18. Anteayer los padres <u>acompañar</u> a su hija al parque.

19. La mamá de él <u>regatear</u> con los vendedores en el mercado.

20. Vincente Flores y Freida Davalos <u>nacer</u> en Cuba en 1722.

Solution to Exercise: The Preterite, Regular Verbs

Rewrite each sentence so that the underlined verb in the infinitive is changed into its correct preterite form.

1. Juan y yo <u>hablamos</u> por teléfono con papá.

2. Ustedes <u>miraron</u> las flores el sábado pasado.

3. Anoche mis nietas me <u>escribieron</u> un correo electrónico.

4. Usted <u>tomó</u> el autobus a las seis de la tarde.

5. Mark nunca <u>peleó</u> el jueves pasado.

6. Su sobrino <u>trabajó</u> en la tienda por un mes.

7. Los médicos <u>entraron</u> a decirnos que era tiempo de salir.

8. Ellas me <u>abrazaron</u> e inmediatamente yo sentía una ola de calma.

9. Tú abriste los ojos a las doce en punto.

10. El gato llegó el año pasado

11. La princesa ofreció una recompensa a los políticos.

12. Los duques valientes rechazaron el rey en 1544.

13. Ella contestó tres preguntas.

14. Las enfermeras llegaron y le hicieron la prueba del alcohol.

15. Miguel terminó el viaje en enero.

16. Cuando Daniel y David salieron del salón de clase, no habían hecho la tarea.

17. Mi novia compró un anillo de oro para mi.

18. Anteayer los padres acompañaron a su hija al parque.

19. La mamá de él regateó con los vendedores en el mercado.

20. Vincente Flores y Freida Davalos nacieron en Cuba en 1722.

Preterite Formation and Use in Irregular Verbs

Objective: Learn how to conjugate and use irregular verbs in the preterite.

Method: Memorize *ser*, *ir*, and *dar*. Memorize the preterite stems of the listed irregular verbs.

Outcome: Correctly complete the exercises that follow.

The Two Basic Sets of Irregular Verbs in the Preterite

1. *Ser*, *ir*, and *dar*.

Ser (to be) and *ir* (to go) share identical preterite forms:

Singular
1. Yo fui = I was/went
2. tú fuiste = you (fam.) were/went

3. él/ella fue = he/she/it was/went
4. usted fue = you (formal) were/went

Plural
5. nosotros/as fuimos = we were/went
6. vosotros/as fuisteis = you were/went (Spain)
7. ellos/as fueron = they were/went
8. ustedes fueron = you were/went

Dar (to give) is an –ar verb but its preterite endings are –er/-ir endings:

<u>Singular</u>

1. Yo di = I gave

2. tú diste = you (fam.) gave

3. él/ella dio = he/she/it gave

4. usted dio = you (formal) gave

<u>Plural</u>

5. nosotros/as dimos = we gave
6. vosotros/as disteis = you gave (Spain)
7. ellos/as dieron = they gave
8. ustedes dieron = you gave

2. Verbs whose preterites are formed by adding preterite endings to their irregular preterite stems:

Infinitive	Stem	Preterite
	Endings	
andar	and<u>uv</u>-	
estar	est<u>uv</u>-	e
poder	p<u>u</u>d-	iste
poner	p<u>us</u>-	o
saber	s<u>up</u>-	o
tener	t<u>u</u>v-	imos
hacer	h<u>ic</u>-	isteis
querer	qu<u>is</u>-	ieron
venir	v<u>in</u>-	ieron
conducir	condu<u>j</u>-	e
decir	di<u>j</u>-	iste
producir	produ<u>j</u>-	o
traducir	tradu<u>j</u>-	o
traer	tra<u>j</u>-	imos
distraer	distra<u>j</u>-	isteis
		eron
		eron

Fig. 4

This is what any two verbs in *Fig. 4*, for example, *poner* (to put) and *decir* (to say), will look like when fully conjugated in the preterite:

130

<u>Singular</u>

1. yo puse = I put

2. tú pusiste = you (fam.) put

3. él/ella puso = he/she/it put

4. usted puso = you (formal) put
<u>Plural</u>
5. nosotros/as pusimos = we put
6. vosotros/as pusisteis = you put (Spain)
7. ellos/as pusieron = they put
8. ustedes pusieron = you put

<u>Singular</u>

1. yo dije = I said

2. tú dijiste = you (fam.) said

3. él/ella dijo = he/she/it said

4. usted dijo = you (formal) said
<u>Plural</u>
5. nosotros/as dijimos = we said
6. vosotros/as dijisteis = you said (Spain)
7. ellos/as dijeron = they said
8. ustedes dijeron = you said

It's easier to remember that all of the verbs cited in *Fig. 4* have **patterns of irregularity**:

    a. None of these verbs carry written accents in their *yo*, *él*, *ella*, or *usted* forms, unlike regular verbs.

b. The verbs *andar, estar, poder, poner, saber,* and *tener* all carry the letter **u** in their preterite stems.

c. The verbs *hacer, querer,* and *venir* all carry the letter **i** in their preterite stems.

d. The verbs *conducir, decir, producir, traducir, traer,* and *distraer* all carry the letter **j** at the end of their preterite stems. They also lose the initial **i** in the *ellos/as,* and *ustedes* parts of the preterite endings.

e. Verbs formed by adding a prefix to any of these irregular verbs will also have the irregular preterite stems belonging to these verbs. For example:

poner→*disponer*→*dispus-*
tener→*detener*→*detuv-*
decir→*predecir*→*predij-*

Exercise : Irregular Preterites

Write the correct preterite form for each underlined item.

1. Yo <u>ir</u> a la fiesta y <u>trajer</u> un postre de flan.

2. Jacobo no <u>hacer</u> la leccion en la clase hoy.

3. Anoche ustedes <u>tener</u> que esperar dos horas sin ella.

4. Mis amigos <u>venir</u> al almuerzo con leche y pan.

5. Miguel y yo no <u>querer</u> viajar en un carro sin luces.

6. Anita me <u>poner</u> una curita despues del accidente.

7. Los artistas <u>producir</u> tres retratos excelentes el mes pasado.

8. ¿<u>Poder</u> ustedes preparar tamales o tostitos?

9. Cuando nosotros <u>saber</u> la verdad ellas <u>llorar</u> otra vez.

10. Ellos <u>andar</u> por la calle para cinco horas.

11. La reina <u>decir</u> que no a la gente.

12. Vosotras <u>traducir</u> facilmente del español al ruso durante el viaje.

13. ¿<u>Conducir</u> Senor Trejo un taxi para treinta años?

14. Vosotros no <u>dar</u> comida al pordiosero tres veces.

15. Para una hora los soldados <u>distraer</u> a los insurgentes con música clásica.

16. Tú no me <u>dar</u> ningún dinero ayer.

17. Él <u>detener</u> el carro en medio del malecón el lunes pasado.

18. Yo <u>estar</u> alegre cuando Perla <u>tener</u> éxito ayer.

19. ¿<u>Ir</u> de compras las familias Villa y Rocha el mes pasado?

20. ¿Quién <u>tener</u> la idea excelente?

Solution to Exercise : Irregular Preterites

1. Yo <u>fui</u> a la fiesta y <u>traje</u> un postre de flan.

2. Jacobo no <u>hizo</u> la lección en la clase hoy.

3. Anoche ustedes <u>tuvieron</u> que esperar dos horas sin ella.

4. Mis amigos <u>vinieron</u> al almuerzo con leche y pan.

5. Miguel y yo no <u>quisimos</u> viajar en un carro sin luces.

6. Anita me <u>puse</u> una curita después del accidente.

7. Los artistas <u>produjeron</u> tres retratos excelentes el mes pasado.

8. ¿<u>Pudieron</u> ustedes preparar tamales o tostitos?

9. Cuando nosotros <u>supimos</u> la verdad ellas <u>lloraron</u> otra vez.

10. Ellos <u>anduvieron</u> por la calle para cinco horas.

11. La reina <u>dijo</u> que no a la gente.

12. Vosotras <u>tradujisteis</u> fácilmente del español al ruso durante el viaje.

13. ¿<u>Condujo</u> el Señor Trejo un taxi para treinta años?

14. Vosotros no <u>disteis</u> comida al pordiosero tres veces.

15. Para una hora los soldados distrajeron a los insurgentes con música clásica.

16.Tú no me diste ningún dinero ayer.

17. Él detuvo el carro en medio del malecón el lunes pasado.

18.Yo estuve alegre cuando Perla tuvo éxito ayer.

19. ¿Fueron de compras las familias Villa y Rocha el mes pasado?

20. ¿Quién tuvo la idea excelente?

The Imperfect

Objective: Learn how to conjugate and use regular verbs in the imperfect.

Method: Memorize a model -*ar,* -*er,* and -*ir* regular verb in the imperfect tense. Memorize the 3 irregular verbs in the imperfect tense.

Outcome: Explain how to change any verb from its infinitive form to its conjugated form in the imperfect. Correctly complete the exercises that follow.

Formation: Regular Verbs

-*ar* verbs: There are 2 basic steps in conjugating a regular **-*ar*** verb, such as *bailar* (to dance), in the imperfect:

1. Drop the infinitive ending of *bailar* and keep the stem *bail*.
2. Add the endings of the imperfect for -*ar* verbs:

Singular: **-*aba*, -*abas*, -*aba*, -*aba***

Plural: **-*ábamos*, -*abais*, -*aban*, -*aban***

that matches what you wish to say or write.

Singular
yo bail***aba*** = I danced
tú bail***abas*** = you (familiar) danced
él/ella bail***aba*** = he/she/it danced
usted bail***aba*** = you (formal) danced
Plural
nosotros/as bail***ábamos*** = we danced
vosotros/as bail***abais*** = you (Spain) danced
ellos/as bail***aban*** = they danced
ustedes bail***aban*** = you danced

-er, -ir verbs: There are 2 basic steps in conjugating a regular **-er** or **-ir** verb, such as *beber* (to drink) or *vivir* (to live), in the imperfect. Note that endings for both **-er** and **-ir** verbs are identical in the imperfect.:

> 1. Drop the infinitive ending of *beber* and keep the stem *beb*. Drop the infinitive ending of *vivir* and keep the stem *viv*.

> 2. Add the endings of the imperfect for **-er** and **-ir** verbs:

Singular: ***-ía, -ías, -ía, -ía***

Plural: ***-íamos, -íais, -ían, -ían***

that matches what you wish to say or write.

Singular
yo beb***ía*** = I drank
tú beb***ías*** = you (familiar) drank
él/ella beb***ía*** = he/she/it drank
usted beb***ía*** = you (formal) drank

nosotros/as beb*íamos* = we drank
vosotros/as beb*íais* = you (Spain) drank
ellos/as beb*ían* = they drank
ustedes beb*ían* = you drank

Singular
yo viv*ía* = I lived
tú viv*ías* = you (familiar) lived
él/ella viv*ía* = he/she/it lived
usted viv*ía* = you (formal) you lived
Plural
nosotros/as viv*íamos* = we lived
vosotros/as viv*íais* = you (Spain) lived
ellos/as viv*ían* = they lived
ustedes viv*ían* = you lived

Irregular Verbs in the Imperfect
There are only three verbs in Spanish that are
irregular in the imperfect. They are *ir* (to go), *ser*
(to be), and *ver* (to see). It might be best to
memorize these 3 verbs.
Singular
yo ib*a* = I went
tú ib*as* = you (familiar) went
él/ella ib*a* = he/she/it went
usted ib*a* = you (formal) went
Plural
nosotros/as *íbamos* = we went
vosotros/as ib*ais* = you (Spain) went
ellos/as ib*an* = they went
ustedes ib*an* = you went

Singular
yo er*a* = I was
tú er*as* = you (familiar) were
él/ella er*a* = he/she/it was
usted er*a* = you (formal) were
Plural
nosotros/as ér*amos* = we were
vosotros/as er*ais* = you (Spain) were
ellos/as er*an* = they were
ustedes er*an* = you were

Singular
yo ve*ía* = I saw
tú ve*ías* = you (familiar) saw
él/ella ve*ía* = he/she/it saw
usted ve*ía* = you (formal) saw
Plural
nosotros/as ve*íamos* = we saw
vosotros/as ve*íais* = you (Spain) saw
ellos/as ve*ían* = they saw
ustedes ve*ían* = you saw

How the Imperfect Is Used

1. To express habitual or repeated actions in the past. Words/expressions such as these often trigger the imperfect: *siempre* (always), *de niño/de niña* (as a child), *todos los días/meses/años* (every day/month/year), *a menudo* (often), *generalmente* (generally). For example:
- *De niña, Marisela siempre jugaba con sus muñecas en la cocina.* (As a child Marisela

always played with her dolls in the kitchen.)

2. To set a scene that creates background description for past actions. For example
- *Era ua día perfecto. El sol brillaba, los pájaros cantaban, y yo comía helado*. (It was a perfect day. The sun was shining, the birds were singing, and I was eating ice cream.)

3. To describe people in the past. For example
- *Felipe Castro era alto, moreno, y muy inteligente.* (Felipe Castro was tall, dark haired, and very smart.)

4. To express time or a date in the past. For example
- *Eran las nueve de la noche.* (It was nine o' clock at night.)
- *Era viernes, el veinticinco de enero.* (It was Friday, January 25th.)

5. To describe an action that was ongoing when another took place to interrupt it. For example
- *David hablaba cuando un perro entró en el cuarto.* (David was speaking when a dog entered the room.)

6. The imperfect is triggered when the conjunction *mientras* links two or more actions taking place at the same time. For example
- *George y yo jugábamos al tenis mientras la familia Rojas daba un vuelta por el parque.* (George and I were playing tennis while the Rojas family strolled in the park.)

7. To describe physical or emotional, states in the past. For example
- *Yo tenía frio.* (I was cold.)
- *Adrianna quería estar feliz con Roberto.* (Adrianna wished to be happy with Roberto.)

8. It describes past action whose beginning or end are either unknown or unimportant. For example
- *Marcelo jugaba con sus amigos.* (Marcelo was playing with his friends.)
- *Erica y Alan comían tacos de pescado.* (Erica and Alan were eating fish tacos.)

Exercise: The Imperfect Indicative

Change all <u>underlined items to</u> the <u>imperfect indicative</u>.

Part A
La clase <u>representa</u> pura confusión. En una esquina un estudiante <u>canta</u> en voz alta, en otra tres alumnas <u>escriben</u> y <u>dibujan</u> en el pizzarón. Dos niños <u>tiran</u> un cuaderno uno al otro mientras la maestra, que <u>es</u> una mujer trabajadora, <u>duerme</u>. Solamente <u>trabaja</u> un estudiante. Lo extraño <u>es</u> que nadie, salvo yo, <u>veo</u> todo esto.

Part B
Afuera, <u>hace</u> buen tiempo. Los perros del vecino <u>ladran</u> porque <u>son</u> felices. Un paletero <u>va</u> de casa en casa para vender sus helados que siempre <u>son</u> sabrosos. Me <u>gusta</u> mas paletas de guanabana. Todos los veranos los niños lo <u>ven</u> o lo _ y siempre <u>van</u> corriendo a su puesto ambulante. Yo <u>recuerdo</u> bien porque siempre lo <u>hago</u> lo mismo.

Part C
Los sábados por la tarde siempre <u>vamos</u> a la misa. Después <u>conducimos</u> a un restaurante mexicano. Mi mamá <u>pide</u> la misma cosa cada vez, albóndigas y sopa con tortillas. Papá <u>prefiere</u> burritos de camarón y yo <u>como</u> tacos de carne asada y <u>bebo</u> horchata. El mesero Pepito <u>es</u> grande, cómico y <u>tiene</u> tatuajes en los brazos. Siempre <u>hay</u> muchos clientes allí y nunca se <u>quejan</u> del servicio o de la comida.

Solution to Exercise: The Imperfect Indicative

Change all of the underlined items to the imperfect indicative.

Part A
La clase representaba pura confusión. En una esquina un estudiante cantaba en voz alta, en otra tres alumnas escribían y dibujaban en el pizzarón. Dos niños tiraban un cuaderno uno al otro mientras la maestra, que era una mujer trabajadora, dormía. Solamente trabajaba un estudiante. Lo extraño era que nadie, salvo yo, veía todo esto.

Part B
Afuera, hacía buen tiempo. Los perros del vecino ladraban porque eran felices. Un paletero iba de casa en casa para vender sus helados que siempre eran sabrosos. Me gustaba más las paletas de guanabana. Todos los veranos los niños lo veían o lo oían y siempre iban corriendo a su puesto ambulante. Yo recordaba bien porque siempre lo hacía lo mismo.

Part C
Los sábados por la tarde siempre íbamos a la misa. Después conducíamos a un restaurante mexicano. Mi mamá pedía la misma cosa cada vez, albóndigas y sopa con tortillas. Papá prefería burritos de camarón y yo comía tacos de carne asada y bebía horchata. El mesero Pepito era grande, cómico y tenía tatuajes en los brazos. Siempre habían muchos clientes allí y nunca se quejaban del servicio o de la comida.

Exercise 2: The Imperfect Indicative

Change all of the <u>underlined items to</u> the <u>imperfect indicative</u>.

1. Todos los años el <u>nadar</u> en la misma playa.

2. De niño yo <u>ir</u> de compras com mi abuela.

3. El agua del lago <u>ser</u> verde, no <u>hacer</u> viento.

4. Martin <u>ser</u> atlético pero Jacobo y Pilar <u>ganar</u> más premios.

5. <u>Ser</u> las dos de la mañana.

6. <u>Ser</u> el doce de junio.

7. Mis hermanas <u>comer</u> cuando se cayó el arbol.

8. Ustedes <u>preparar</u> tamales y tostitos.

9. Las niñas <u>saltar</u> la cuerda mientras los niños <u>jugar</u> al fútbol.

10. Yo <u>montar</u> en bicicleta mientras mis amigos <u>leer</u> sus libros.

11. Las muchachas <u>tener</u> frío pero yo <u>querer</u> estar en Puerto Rico durante el invierno.

12. El Señor Fox y su hija <u>tocar</u> el piano, yo <u>oir</u> la música y <u>bailar</u> el tango.

13. Mis abuelitos me <u>dar</u> regalitos y mi hermano mayor siempre me los <u>quitar</u>.

14. Tú querer vender la bicicleta.

15. Mi amigo creer que ella ser cómica.

16. Nosotros hablar francés todos los días.

Solutions to Exercise 2: The Imperfect Indicative

Change all of the <u>underlined items to</u> the <u>imperfect indicative</u>.

1. Todos los años el <u>nadaba</u> en la misma playa.

2. De niño yo <u>iba</u> de compras com mi abuela.

3. El agua del lago <u>era</u> verde, no <u>hacía</u> viento.

4. Martin <u>era</u> atlético pero Jacobo y Pilar <u>ganaban</u> más premios.

5. <u>Eran</u> las dos de la mañana.

6. <u>Era</u> el doce de junio.

7. Mis hermanas <u>comían</u> cuando se cayó el arbol.

8. Ustedes <u>preparaba</u> tamales y tostitos.

9. Las niñas <u>saltaban</u> la cuerda mientras los niños <u>jugaban</u> al fútbol.

10. Yo <u>montaba</u> en bicicleta mientras mis amigos <u>leían</u> sus libros.

11. Las muchachas <u>tenían</u> frío pero yo <u>quería</u> estar en Puerto Rico durante el invierno.

12. El Señor Fox y su hija <u>tocaban</u> el piano, yo <u>oía</u> la música y <u>bailaba</u> el tango.

13. Mis abuelitos me <u>daban</u> regalitos y mi hermano mayor siempre me los <u>quitaba</u>.

14. Tú <u>querías</u> vender la bicicleta.

15. Mi amigo <u>creía</u> que ella <u>era</u> cómica.

16. Nosotros <u>hablábamos</u> francés todos los días.

Part 5

Reflexive Verbs in the
Present Indicative

Reflexive Verbs

Objective: Demonstrate understanding of reflexive action in Spanish verbs.
Method: Memorize a model *reflexive verb*. Demonstrate how it is used in speaking and writing.
Outcome: Explain how to change any reflexive verb from its infinitive form to its conjugated form. Correctly complete the exercises that follow.

A reflexive verb represents an action that a person or thing performs on himself or itself. Put another way, the action affects the doer of the action (the subject) and does not pass to an outside recipient of the action (or object).

In English, reflexive verbs are followed by the following words: *myself, yourself, himself, herself, itself, ourselves, themselves, yourselves*. For example
-I look at **myself** in the mirror.
-They dress **themselves** every morning.

In Spanish we recognize a reflexive verb by its marker *se*. For example
-*levantarse* (to get up)
-*despedirse* (to say goodbye)
Reflexive verbs are conjugated like any other Spanish verbs except that they also carry the

reflexive pronouns:
Singular : me, te, se
Plural : nos, os, se

Here are two samples of fully conjugated reflexive verbs in the present indicative:
Levantarse (to get up)

Singular
Yo *me* levanto = I get up
tú *te* levantas = you (familiar) get up
él/ella *se* levanta = he/she/it gets up
usted *se* levanta = you (formal) get up
Plural
nosotros/as *nos* levantamos = we get up
vosotros/as *os* levantáis = you (Spain) get up
ellos/as *se* levantan = they get up
ustedes *se* levantan = you get up

Aburrirse (to be/become bored)

Singular
Yo *me* aburro = I am bored
tú *te* aburres = you (familiar) are bored
él/ella *se* aburre = he/she/it is bored
usted *se* aburre = you (formal) are bored
Plural
nosotros/as *nos* aburrimos = we are bored
vosotros/as *os* aburrís = you (Spain) are bored
ellos/as *se* aburren = they are bored
ustedes *se* aburren = you are bored

Uses of Reflexive Verbs

1. To depict an action performed on oneself. For example
- *Me afeito a las ocho.* (I shave myself at 8 o'clock).
- *Ella se baña dos veces por dia.* (She takes a bath twice a day.)

2. To depict reciprocal action. For example
- *Mari y Alán se compran regalos cada mes.* (Mari and Alan buy each other gifts every month).
- *Ellos se escriben mensajes en clase.* (They write each other messages in class.)

3. When the speaker or writer does not directly say who or what is doing the action. In other words, as a substitute for the passive voice. For example
- *Se hablan español aquí.* (Spanish is spoken here).
- *Se venden leche en la tienda.* (Milk is sold in the store.)

4. Some verbs are used idiomatically since they have a different meaning in their reflexive form. For example
- *burlar* (to decieve) **but** *burlase de* (to make fun of)
- *poner* (to put) **but** *ponerse* (to put on).

5. The reflexive construction with *se* is used with the verb in the third person singular (or the *él/ella* part of the verb) to convey a sense of the English *one*, or *they*. For example

- *Se puede tomar café toda la noche.* (One can drink coffee all night).
- *Se dice que ella es famosa en España.* (They say she is famous in Spain.)

6. Most verbs can be used without reflexive pronouns. When this happens, the action passes from the person or thing doing the action to another person or thing receiving the action. For example

-*Señora Chavez se despierta* (Mrs. Chavez wakes up.) **but** *Señora Chavez despierta a su bebé* (Mrs. Chavez wakes up her baby.)

- *El hombre se cepilla el pelo* (the man brushes his hair.) **but** *El hombre cepilla a su perro* (the man brushes his dog).

Exercises: Reflexive Verbs

Change all <u>underlined reflexive verbs in</u> their infinitive forms to their conjugated present indicative forms

Exercise A

Hola! Yo **llamarse** Gabriel Cepeda y tengo quince años. Hoy hablo de mi rutina diaria. **Despertarse** (e>ie) a las cuatro de la mañana pero **levantarse** más tarde a las cinco y media. **Cepillarse** los dientes y **desayunarse** un sanwich de jamón y queso, jugo de naranja, y cereal. Poco después **afietarse**, **quitarse** la ropa, y **ducharse**. No **maquillarse** pero mi hermana, Leonora, **lavarse** la cara y **maquillarse** pasando horas en el baño. Yo **secarse**, **ponerse** la ropa y digo adiós a

mi mamá. Salgo para la escuela. Yo regreso a la

casa a las cuatro y **acostarse** (o>ue) a las nueve y media. Ahorita no **enamorarse** de nadie. Tal vez va a pasar en el futuro.

Solution to Exercises: Reflexive Verbs

Change all <u>underlined reflexive verbs in their infinitive forms to their conjugated present indicative forms</u>

Exercise A

Hola! Yo **me llamo** Gabriel Cepeda y tengo quince años. Hoy hablo de mi rutina diaria. **Me despierto** (e>ie) a las cuatro de la mañana pero **me levanto** más tarde a las cinco y media. **Me cepillo** los dientes y **me desayuno** un sanwich de jamón y queso, jugo de naranja, y cereal. Poco después **me afieto**, **me quito** la ropa, y **me ducho**. No **me maquillo** pero mi hermana, Leonora, **se lava** la cara y **se maquilla** pasando horas en el baño. Yo **me seco**, **me pongo** la ropa y digo adiós a mi

mamá. Salgo para la escuela. Yo regreso a la casa a las cuatro y **me acuesto** a las nueve y media. Ahorita no **me enamoro** de nadie. Tal vez va a pasar en el futuro.

Exercise B
Create sentences using the following information
1. Yo / lavarse / los pies.
2. Miguel y Gregorio / desayunarse / en casa.

3. Ella no / maquillarse / todos los días.

4. Mi amigo / ponerse / el abrigo.
5. las ninas / secarse / las manos.
6. Sara y yo / sentarse / en los asientos.
7. Mis hermanos / probarse / los sombreros.
8. Hola, nosotros / llamarse / los tres amigos.

9. ¿ Bañarse / tú / con agua caliente?

10. Yo no / quedarse / solito en casa.
11. Mi perrito nunca/ enfermarse / en el carro.

Exercise C
Rewrite the following sentences using the reflexive pronouns only where necessary.
1. Mario lavarse la cara.
2. Carlos lavarse al perro.
3. Maribel secarse los pies.
4. Carla secarse a su hermanito.
5. Los peluqueros afietarse.
6. Nosotros acostarse a las once.
7. Yo cepillarse los dientes a mi hijo.
8. Monica levantarse la silla.
9. Isac y su perro levantarse temprano.
10. Ellos sentarse en la clase.

Solution to: *Exercise B*

Create sentences using the following information
1. Yo me lavo los pies.
2. Miguel y Gregorio se desayunan en casa.

3. Ella no se maquilla todos los días.

4. Mi amigo se pone el abrigo.
5. las niñas se secan las manos.
6. Sara y yo nos sentamos en los asientos.
7. Mis hermanos se prueban los sombreros.
8. Hola, nosotros nos llamamos los tres amigos.

9. ¿ Te bañas tú con agua caliente?

10. Yo no me quedo solito en casa.
11. Mi perrito nunca se enferma en el carro.

Solution to: *Exercise C*

Rewrite the following sentences using the reflexive pronouns only where necessary.
1. Mario se lava la cara.
2. Carlos lava al perro.
3. Maribel se seca los pies.
4. Carla seca a su hermanito.
5. Los peluqueros se afietan.
6. Nosotros nos acostamos a las once.
7. Yo cepillo los dientes a mi hijo.
8. Monica levanta la silla.
9. Isac y su perro se levantan temprano.
10. Ellos se sentan en la clase.

Partial Word Bank for 3 Types of Reflexive Verbs

Verbs of daily routine

acostarse	to go to bed
afeitarse	to shave
bañarse	to take a bath
cepillarse	to brush (hair, teeth)
cortarse	to cut (hair, nails)
desayunarse	to have breakfast
despertarse	to wake up
lavararse	to wash up
levantarse	to get up
maquillarse	to put on makeup
peinarse	to comb one's hair
ponerse	to put on (clothes)
quitarse	to take off (clothes)
secarse	to dry oneself
vestirse	to get dressed

Verbs that signal a sudden change of state or emotion

alegrarse	to become happy
enamorarse	to fall in love
enfermarse	to become sick
enojarse,	to become angry
enfadarse	to become angry
entristecerse	to become sad
dormirse	to fall asleep
morirse	to die (suddenly)

Verbs that have a different meaning in their reflexive and non-reflexive forms

abonarse	to subscribe
abonar	to credit
acostarse	to go to bed
acostar	to lay down
alegrarse	to be glad
alegrar	to liven up
burlarse de	to make fun of
burlar	to deceive
contentarse	to be satisfied
contentar	to please
encontrarse con	to meet
encontrar	to find
fijarse	to pay attention
fijar	to fix in place
irse	to leave
ir	to go
pasarse de	to exceed
pasar	to pass
volverse	to become, to turn
volver	to return

Part 6

Special Topics: Time, Family, Cognates, Agreement, Clothing and Colors

Telling Time

Objective: Learn how to tell time on the clock.

Method: Understand conventions used in telling time through written and oral practice.

Outcome: Demonstrate mastery by correctly completing exercises that follow on time problems.

This lesson is divided into three segments. The first segment deals with how we call the hours. The second segment deals with how we call the hours combined with minutes 1 through 30. The third segment deals with how we call the hours combined with minutes 31 through 59.

The hours

To say it is 1o'clock
-*Es la una.*
To say it is 2 o'clock
-*Son las dos.*
To say it is 11 o'clock
-*Son las once.*

Anytime there is a reference to one o' clock, start the sentence with *Es la*. Whenever there is reference to any other number, start the sentence with **Son las**. Seven o' clock, for instance would be *Son las siete*.

Hours Combined with Minutes 1 through 30

In this instance, minutes 1-30 are on the **Y**-side (and) of the clock. Therefore:

1:02 will be: *Es la una y dos*.

1:13 will be: *Es la una y trece*.

4:10 will be: *Son las cuatro y diez*.

10:28 will be: *Son las diez y veintiocho*.

Hours Combined with Minutes 31 through 59

In this instance, minutes 31-59 are on the **Menos** side (before/to) of the clock. Follow these steps when calling time on the menos side of the clock using a time of 1:31:

1. add 1 to the hour making it 2
2. Subtract 31 from 60 (60 – 31 = 29)
3. We now have two new numbers that we will line up in the above order and insert menos in the middle: 2 menos 29.

The time will be *Son las dos **menos** veintinueve*. Using the same approach, 1:42 will be: *Son las dos **menos** dieciocho*.

8:50 will be: *Son las nueve **menos** diez*.

Think of time on the menos side of the clock in terms of ***minutes before the hour or to the hour*** as in 18 minutes before two instead of 1:42 or as 10 minutes before nine instead of 50 minutes after 8.

Additional Time Facts

Quarter past the hour is often expressed as **y cuarto** as in:
1:15 = Es la una y cuarto.
7:15 = Son las siete y cuarto.
Quarter to the hour is often expressed as **menos cuarto** as in:
1:45 = Son las dos menos cuarto.
7:45 = Son las ocho menos cuarto.
Half past the hour is often expressed as **y media** as in:
9:30 = Son las nueve y media.
12:30 = Son las doce y media.
To have a clearer idea of which 12 o' clock is intended, we have the espressions:

Es mediodía (It's midday).

Es medianoche (It's midnight).

To have a clearer idea of which part of the day is intended, we have the expressions:
de la mañana (In the morning or a.m.).
de la tarde (In the afternoon or p.m).
de la noche (at night)

At the hour is often expressed as *A la* or *a las* as in:
At 9:20 = A las nueve y veinte.
At 6:30 = A las seis y media.

Exercise: Telling time

The hours

Model: 7: 00 <u>Son las siete.</u>

1. 2:00 _____.
2. 11:00 _____.
3. 1:00 _____.
4. 6:00 _____.
5. 9:00 _____.
6. 3:00 _____.
7. 12:00 _____.
8. 9:00 _____.
9. 5:00 _____.
10. 4:00 _____.

Hours combined with minutes 1through 30

1. 12:01 _____.
2. 3:07 _____.
3. 9:20 _____.
4. 11:09 _____.
5. 6:14 _____.
6. 5:19 _____.
7. 8:27 _____.
8. 7:13 _____.
9. 2:05 _____.
10. 5:10 _____.

Hours combined with minutes 31through 59

1. 5:40 _____.
2. 3:55 _____.
3. 12:35 _____.
4. 7:31 _____.
5. 11:44 _____.
6. 2:38 _____.
7. 9:36 _____.
8. 10:50 _____.
9. 6:58 _____.
10. 1:48 _____.

Time combo

1. 6:00 _____.
2. 7:30 _____.
3. 12:45 _____.
4. 9:27 a.m. _____.
5. 3:15 _____.
6. At 9:50 _____.
7. 11:30 p.m. _____.
8. 5:53 _____.
9. 12:00 midday _____.
10. 1:09 p.m. _____.
11. 6:15 a.m. _____.
12. At 3:10 _____.

Solutions to Exercise: Telling time

The hours

Model: 7: 00 <u>Son las siete.</u>

1. 2:00   <u>Son las dos.</u>
2. 11:00   <u>Son las once.</u>
3. 1:00   <u>Es la una.</u>
4. 6:00   <u>Son las seis</u>
5. 9:00   <u>Son las nueve.</u>
6. 3:00   <u>Son las tres.</u>
7. 12:00   <u>Son las doce.</u>
8. 9:00   <u>Son las nueve.</u>
9. 5:00   <u>Son las cinco</u>
10. 4:00   <u>Son las cuatro.</u>

Hours combined with minutes 1through 30

1. 12:01   <u>Son las doce y uno.</u>
2. 3:07   <u>Son las tres y siete.</u>
3. 9:20   <u>Son las nueve y veinte.</u>
4. 11:09   <u>Son las once y nueve.</u>
5. 6:14   <u>Son las seis y catorce.</u>
6. 5:19   <u>Son las cinco y diecinueve.</u>
7. 8:27   <u>Son las ocho y veintinueve.</u>
8. 7:13   <u>Son las siete y trece.</u>
9. 2:05   <u>Son las dos y cinco.</u>
10. 5:10   <u>Son las cinco y diez.</u>

Hours combined with minutes 31through 59

1. 5:40   Son las seis menos veinte.
2. 3:55   Son las cuatro menos cinco.
3. 12:35   Es la una menos veinticinco.
4. 7:31   Son las ocho menos veintinueve.
5. 11:44   Son las doce menos dieciséis.
6. 2:38   Son las tres menos veintidós.
7. 9:36   Son las diez menos veinticuatro.
8. 10:50   Son las once menos diez.
9. 6:58   Son las siete menos dos.
10. 1:48   Son las dos menos doce.

Time combo

1. 6:00 Son las seis.
2. 7:30 Son las siete y media.
3. 12:45 Es la una y cuarto.
4. 9:27 a.m. Son las diez y veintisiete de la mañana.
5. 3:15 Son las tres y cuarto.
6. At 9:50 A las diez menos diez.
7. 11:30 p.m. Son las once y media de la tarde.
8. 5:53 Son las seis menos siete.
9. 12:00 midday Es mediodía.
10. 1:09 p.m. Es la una y nueve de la tarde.
11. 6:15 a.m. Son las seis y cuarto de la mañana.
12. At 3:10 A las tres y diez.

La Familia

Objective: Give a brief explanation of each vocabulary term given in this lesson.
Method: Use vocabulary in written and oral practice.
Outcome: Demonstrate mastery by correctly completing exercises that follow.

The second special topic deals with human relationships based on family. The vocabulary that follows covers most of the words commonly used to describe relatives in the Western world. The exercise that follows the vocabulary list is formatted to challenge the student not only to master the vocabulary item, but, more importantly, to explain what each term means.

great grandmother	la bisabuela
great grandfather	el bisabuelo
grandmother	la abuela
grandfather	el abuelo
grandparents	los abuelos
granddaughter	la nieta
grandson	el nieto
mother	la madre, la mamá
father	el padre, el papá
parents	los padres
husband	el esposo
wife	la esposa

married couple	los esposos
stepmother	la madrastra
stepfather	el padrastro
child	el hijo, la hija
children	los hijos
son	el hijo
daughter	la hija
brother	el hermano
sister	la hermana
step brother	el hermanastro
step sister	la hermanastra
brother-in-law	el cuñado
sister-in-law	la cuñada
relatives	los parientes
aunt	la tía
uncle	el tío
cousin (male)	el primo
cousin (female)	la prima
cousins	los primos
niece	la sobrina
nephew	el sobrino
nieces and nephews	los sobrinos
daughter-in-law	la nuera
son-in-law	el yerno
father-in-law	el suegro
mother-in-law	la suegra

Exercise: La Familia

Fill in each blank with the correct word.

1. La mamá de mi abuela es mi _____.
2. El papá de mi abuela es mi _____.
3. La mamá de mi mamá es mi _____.
4. El papá de mi papá es mi _____.
5. Los padres de mis padres son mis _____.
6. La hija de mi hijo/a es mi _____.
7. El hijo de mi hijo/a es mi _____.
8. La esposa de mi papá es mi _____.
9. El esposo de mi mamá es mi _____.
10. La mamá de mi nieto/a es mi _____.
11. El papá de mis hijos es mi _____.
12. La mamá de mis hijos es mi _____.
13. La esposa de mi papá es mi _____.
14. El esposo de mi mamá es mi _____.
15. El papá de mi nieto/a es mi _____.
16. Los hijos de mi esposo/a son mis <u>hijos</u>.
17. El hijo de mi esposo/a es mi _____.
18. La hija de mi esposo/a es mi _____.
19. El hijo de mis padres es mi _____.
20. La hija de mis padres es mi _____.
21. El hijo de mi padrastro/madrastra es mi _____.
22. La hija de mi padrastro/madrastra es mi _____.
23. El hermano de mi esposa es mi _____.
24. La hermana de mi esposo es mi _____.
25. Leave blank

26. La hermana de mi mamá/papá es mi _____.
27. El hermano de mi mamá/papá es mi _____.
28. El hijo de mi tío/tia es mi _____.
29. La hija de mi tío/tia es mi _____.
30. Los hijos de mis tíos/tías son mis _____.
31. La hija de mi hermano/a es mi _____.
32. El hijo de mi hermano/a es mi _____.
33. Los hijos de mis hermanos son mis _____.
34. El papá de mi esposo/a es mi _____.
35. La mamá de mi esposo/a es mi _____.
36. El esposo de mi hija es mi _____.
37. La esposa de mi hijo es mi _____.

Solutions to Exercise: La Familia

1. La mamá de mi abuela es mi <u>bisabuela</u>.
2. El papá de mi abuela es mi <u>bisabuelo</u>.
3. La mamá de mi mamá es mi <u>abuela</u>.
4. El papá de mi papá es mi <u>abuelo</u>.
5. Los padres de mis padres son mis <u>abuelos</u>.
6. La hija de mi hijo/a es mi <u>nieta</u>.
7. El hijo de mi hijo/a es mi <u>nieto</u>.
8. La esposa de mi papá es mi <u>mamá</u>.
9. El esposo de mi mamá es mi <u>papá</u>.
10. La mamá de mi nieto/a es mi <u>hija</u>.
11. El papá de mis hijos es mi <u>esposo</u>.
12. La mamá de mis hijos es mi <u>esposa</u>.
13. La esposa de mi papá es mi <u>madrastra</u>.
14. El esposo de mi mamá es mi <u>padrastro</u>.
15 El papá de mi nieto/a es mi <u>hijo</u>.
16. Los hijos de mi esposo/a son mis <u>hijos</u>.
17. El hijo de mi esposo/a es mi <u>hijo</u>.
18. La hija de mi esposo/a es mi <u>hija</u>.
19. El hijo de mis padres es mi <u>hermano</u>.
20. La hija de mis padres es mi <u>hermana</u>.
21. El hijo de mi padrastro/madrastra es mi <u>hermanastro</u>.
22. La hija de mi padrastro/madrastra es mi <u>hermanastra</u>.
23. El hermano de mi esposa es mi <u>cuñado</u>.
24. La hermana de mi esposo es mi <u>cuñada</u>.
25. Leave blank
26. La hermana de mi mamá/papá es mi <u>tía</u>.
27. El hermano de mi mamá/papá es mi <u>tío</u>.

28. El hijo de mi tío/tía es mi <u>primo</u>.
29. La hija de mi tío/tía es mi <u>prima</u>.
30. Los hijos de mis <u>tíos/ tías</u> son mis <u>primos</u>.
31. La hija de mi hermano/a es mi <u>sobrina</u>.
32. El hijo de mi hermano/a es mi <u>sobrino</u>.
33. Los hijos de mis hermanos son mis <u>sobrinos</u>.
34. El papá de mi esposo/a es mi <u>suegro</u>.
35. La mamá de mi esposo/a es mi <u>suegra</u>.
36. El esposo de mi hija es mi <u>yerno</u>.
37. La esposa de mi hijo es mi <u>nuera</u>.

Cognates

Objective: Learn what cognates are and how they are used.
Method: Practice written and/or oral exercises.
Outcome: Demonstrate mastery by correctly completing exercises that follow on cognate problems.

A cognate is a word that **looks the same** or almost the same and **means the same** in English as it does in Spanish. Examples of cognates are *color*, *estimar*, and *normalmente*.

Cognates are words that generally **come from earlier root forms such as Greek or Latin** and have made their way into English and Spanish and **retain the same or similar meanings** in both languages.

Fig. 5 below summarizes how English suffixes change into Spanish suffixes for cognate adjectives, nouns, and adverbs:

English	Spanish
-ary imaginary	*-rio imaginario*
-nt ignorant	*-nte ignorante*
-id solid	*-ido sólido*
-ile fragile	*-il frágil*
-ive narrative	*-ivo narrativo*
-ous curious	*-oso curioso*
-ic romantic	*-ico romántico*
-dent president	*-dente presidente*
-gy geology	*-ía geología*
-ism tourism	*-ismo turismo*
-cy decency	*-cia decencia*
-ment monument	*-mento monumento*
-nce experience	*-ncia experiencia*
-ry salary	*-rio salario*

Fig. 5

-tude attitude	*-itud actitud*
-ty trinity	*-dad trinidad*
-y theory	*-ía teoría*
-ist artist	*-ista artista*
-tion action	*-ción acción*
-ly generally	*-mente generalmente*

Fig.5 (cont'd)

We will discuss cognates under 5 categories:

1. *Adjectives* that end with

-ible:	posible	visible	horrible
-al:	principal	normal	natural
-rior:	interior	superior	inferior
-ico:	elástico	fantástico	romántico
-oso:	curioso	famoso	delicioso
-ivo:	narrativo	objetivo	paliativo
-rio:	imaginario	ordinario	monetario
-ente:	decente	inteligente	paciente
-co:	político	logico	práctico

2. *Noun*s that end with

-or:	motor	doctor	horror
-ción:	emoción	acción	atención

-sión: ilusión   explosión   invasión

-al: animal   canal   capital
-ía: teoría   biología   geología
-ista: dentista   artista   terrorista

-mento: monumento   fragmento
         testamento
-dad: actividad   dignidad   trinidad
-ismo: turismo   socialismo
         capitalismo
-itud: actitud   altitud   latitud
-rio: laboratorio   salario   canario
-a: poema   problema   emblema
-ente: agente   presidente   accidente
-cia: urgencia   decencia   agencia (cy)
         distancia   Alicia   ciencia (ce)

3. _Adverbs_ that end with
 -mente:

correctamente   generalmente
posiblemente   sinceramente
normalmente   exactamente
absolutamente   finalmente

4. *Verbs*

The majority of Spanish verbs end with *-ar*. The *-ar* ending carries the English meaning of "to", for example entr**ar** meaning "**to** enter." Many of these *-ar* verbs are cognates.

Fig. 6 below summarizes how English suffixes change into Spanish suffixes for cognate verbs:

English	*Spanish*
-ate accelerate	*-ar acelerar*

Vowel +consonant + t
  -ult   insult
  -ent   present
  -ort   import
 	
  -ist   insist
	-ar { *insultar*
	presentar
	importar
	
	-ir insistir

Vowel +consonant + e
  -use abuse
  -yze analyze
  -ire admire
  -ore explore
	-ar { *abusar*
	analizar
	admirar
	explorar

-ify simplify	*-ificar simplificar*

Fig. 6

Here is a partial list of verb cognates.

-ate accelerate → **-ar acelerar**

Similar verb cognates:

Demonstrate → demonstrar

recuperate → recuperar

liberate → liberar

estimate → estimar

-ult insult → **-ar insultar**

Similar verb cognates:

consult → consultar

exault → exaltar

assault → asaltar

-ort import → **-ar iportar**

Similar verb cognates:

export → exportar

import → importar

support → soportar

-ist insist → **-ir insistir**

Similar verb cognates:

exist → existir

persist → persistr

assist → asistir

-use abuse → **-ar abusar**

Similar verb cognates:

accuse → acusar

cause → causar

recuse → recusar

-ore adore → **-ar adorar**
Similar verb cognates:
> deplore → deplorar
> explore → explorar
> implore → implorar

-ify simplify → **-ar simplificar**
Similar verb cognates:
> classify → clasificar
> dignify → dignificar
> deify → deificar
> unify → unificar

5. _False Cognates_ These words **may look the same** or almost the same **but have different meanings** in English and Spanish. Here is a partial list:

asistir	to attend(school)
come	he/she/it eats
el pie	foot (anatomy)
dime	tell me
constipado	congested (from a cold)
embarazo	pregnancy
la libreria	bookstore
sin	without
los males	evils
la desgracia	misfortune, bad luck
sensible	sensitive
revolver	to mix
simpático	nice (personality)
el pastel	cake

el collar	necklace
leer	to read
quince	fifteen
la ropa	clothing
tan	so
un rato	a while

Exercise: Write in the Adjective Cognates

Fill in the blanks with the correct Spanish adjective cognates.

English	Spanish
active	
festive	
brutal	
delicious	
porous	
electric	
automatic	
terrible	
notable	
convenient	
lucid	
solid	
ordinary	
important	

Fig. 7

Exercise: Write in the Noun Cognates

Fill in the blanks with the correct English noun cognates.

Spanish	English
actor	
doctor	
dictador	
hospital	
moral	
dentista	
comunista	
pesimista	

Fig. 8

idealismo	
mecanismo	
experiencia	
universidad	
condición	
urgencia	
diccionario	

Fig. 8(cont'd)

Exercise: Write in the Adverb Cognates

Fill in the blanks with the correct Spanish and English adverb cognates.

English	Spanish
gracefully	
	naturalmente
	efectivamente
absolutely	
finally	
patiently	
	correctamente
actively	
	prudentamente
	exactamente
	sinceramente
practically	
rapidly	
	normalmente
constantly	

Fig. 9

Exercise A: Write in the Verb Cognates

Fill in the blanks with the correct English verb cognates. Circle the *-ar* and *-ir* endings of each Spanish verb and write *to* in front of each English verb to show they have the same meaning.

Spanish	English
demonstrar	
estimar	
adaptar	
operar	
fermentar	
comportar	
insistir	
existir	
declarar	
civilizar	
deplorar	
paralizar	
excusar	
clasificar	
pacificar	

Fig. 10

Exercise B: Write in the Verb Cognates

Fill in the blanks with the correct Spanish verb cognates.

English	Spanish
to liberate	
to associate	
to participate	
to represent	
to lament	
to accuse	
to compare	
to analyze	
to deplore	
to escape	
to imagine	
to unify	
to modify	
to justify	
to communicate	

Fig. 11

Exercise: Blended Cognate Activity

Fill in the blanks with the correct English or Spanish cognates for nouns, adjectives, adverbs, and verbs.

English	Spanish
fragile	
	agregar
	gratificar
marvellously	
	composición
	indicativo
to pass	
mobile	
silently	
	unificar
ignorant	
	lógicamente
to invite	
	superior
	exempción

Fig. 12

189

Solutions to Exercise: Write in the Adjective Cognates

Fill in the blanks with the correct Spanish adjective cognates.

English	Spanish
active	**activo**
festive	**festivo**
brutal	**brutal**
delicious	**delicioso**
porous	**poroso**
electric	**eléctrico**
automatic	**automático**
terrible	**terrible**
notable	**notable**
convenient	**conveniente**
lucid	**lucido**
solid	**sólido**
ordinary	**ordinario**
important	**importante**

Fig. 13

Solutions to Exercise: Write in the Noun Cognates

Fill in the blanks with the correct English noun cognates.

Spanish	English
actor	**actor**
doctor	**doctor**
dictador	**dictator**
hospital	**hospital**
moral	**moral**
dentista	**dentist**
comunista	**communist**
pesimista	**pessimist**
idealismo	**idealism**

Fig. 14

mecanismo	**mechanism**
experiencia	**experience**
universidad	**university**
condición	**condition**
urgencia	**urgency**
diccionario	**dictionary**

Fig. 14(cont'd)

Solutions to Exercise: Write in the Adverb Cognates

Fill in the blanks with the correct Spanish and English adverb cognates.

English	Spanish
gracefully	**graciosamente**
naturally	**naturalmente**
efectively	efectivamente
absolutely	**absolutamente**
finally	**finalmente**
patiently	**pacientamente**
correctly	correctamente
actively	**activamente**
prudently	prudentamente
exactly	exactamente
sincerely	sinceramente
practically	**practicamante**
rapidly	**rapidamente**
normally	normalmente
constantly	**constantamente**

Fig. 15

Solutions to Exercise A: Write in the Verb Cognates

Fill in the blanks with the correct English verb cognates. Circle the *-ar* and *-ir* endings of each Spanish verb and write *to* in front of each English verb to show they have the same meaning.

Spanish	English
demonstrar	**to demonstrate**
estimar	**to estimate**
adaptar	**to adapt**
operar	**to operate**
fermentar	**to ferment**
comportar	**to comport**
insistir	**to insist**
existir	**to exist**
declarar	**to declare**
civilizar	**to civilize**
deplorar	**to deplore**
paralizar	**to paralyze**
excusar	**to excuse**
clasificar	**to classify**
pacificar	**pacify**

Fig. 16

194

Solutions to Exercise B: Write in the Verb Cognates

Fill in the blanks with the correct Spanish verb cognates.

English	Spanish
to liberate	**liberar**
to associate	**asociar**
to participate	**participar**
to represent	**representar**
to lament	**lamentar**
to accuse	**acusar**
to compare	**comparar**
to analyze	**analizar**
to deplore	**deplorar**
to escape	**escapar**
to imagine	**imaginar**
to unify	**unificar**
to modify	**modificar**
to justify	**justificar**
to communicate	**comunicar**

Fig. 17

Solutions to Exercise: Blended Cognate Activity
Fill in the blanks with the correct English or
Spanish cognates for nouns, adjectives, adverbs,
and verbs.

English	Spanish
fragile	**frágil**
to add	agregar
to gratify	gratificar
marvellously	**maravillosamente**
composition	composición
indicative	indicativo
to pass	**pasar**
mobile	**móvil**
silently	**silenciosamente**
to unify	unificar
ignorant	**ignorante**
logically	lógicamente
to invite	**invitar**
superior	superior
exemption	exempción

Fig. 18

196

Noun-Adjective Agreement

Objective: Learn how adjectives are applied to the nouns they describe.

Method: Practice written and/or oral exercises.

Outcome: Demonstrate mastery by correctly completing exercises that follow on noun-adjective agreement.

Definitions

    A noun is the name of a person(Mary), animal(the cow), place (San Diego), thing (the car), or idea (beauty, honor, truth).

    An adjective is a word that describes a noun. Examples of adjectives are funny, gentle, beautiful, yellow, simple.

    In Spanish, singular nouns take singular adjectives, plural nouns take plural adjectives, masculine nouns take masculine adjectives and feminine nouns take feminine adjectives.

Masculine Singular	*Masculine Plural*
el chico alto	los chicos altos
(the tall boy)	(the tall boys)
el hombre famoso	los hombres
famosos.	
(the famous man)	(the famous
men)	men)

el carro rojo　　　　　　　los carros rojos
　(the red car)　　　　　　　(the red cars.)
Most masculine nouns end in *o* and most of the
adjectives that describe them also end in *o*. A
singular masculine noun takes a singular masculine
adjective. Plural masculine nouns take plural
masculine adjectives. This ***matching up between
noun and adjective*** in gender and number is ***called
noun-adjective agreement***.

Feminine Singular	***Feminine Plural***
la chica alta	las chicas altas.
(the tall girl)	(the tall girls)
la mujer famosa.	las mujeres famosas.
(the famous woman.)	(the famous
women)	
la puerta roja	las puertas rojas
(the red door)	(the red doors)

Most feminine nouns end in *a* and most of the
adjectives that describe them also end in *a*. A
singular feminine noun takes a singular feminine
adjective. Plural feminine noun takes a plural
feminine adjective. This ***matching up between
noun and adjective*** in gender and number is ***called
noun-adjective agreement***.

<u>Exceptions</u>

The adjectives that follow have a ***singular and
plural form only***. They apply to either the
feminine or masculine gender.

Adjectives that end in *e* have singular and plural forms only:

Singular	*Plural*
inteligente	inteligentes
grande	grandes
triste	tristes
verde	verdes

Examples: -*El chico inteligente (the smart boy)*
-*La chica inteligente (the smart girl)*
-*Los chicos inteligentes (the smart boys)*
-*Las chicas inteligentes (the smart girls)*

Adjectives that end in *l* have singular and plural forms only:

Singular	*Plural*
azul	azules
fácil,	fáciles
difícil	díficiles
útil,	útiles

Examples: -*El carro azul (the blue car)*
-*La mujer difícil (the difficult woman)*
-*Los carros azules (the blue cars)*
-*Las mujeres difíciles (the difficult women)*

Adjectives that end in *or* have singular and plural forms only:

Singular	*Plural*
exterior	exteriores

interior   interiores
mayor   mayores
peor   peores

Examples:

-El hermano mayor (the older brother)
-La hermana mayor (the older sister)
-Los hermanos mayores (the older brothers)
-Las hermanas mayores (the older sisters)

Adjectives that end in **on** have singular and plural forms only:

Singular   **Plural**
marrón   marrones
pelón   pelones

The Placement of Adjectives

Adjectives generally follow nouns in Spanish. For example:

la casa roja (the red house)
los libros nuevos. (the new books)

There are two instances when adjectives go in front of the noun:

1. When the adjective is one of quantity.

mucho dinero   *poco café*
  (much money)   (little coffee)
muchas rosas   *pocos ninos*
  (many roses)   (few children)

2. When the adjective is one of number.

tres estudiantes   (three students)

diez manzanas   (ten apples)

Some adjectives have different meanings depending on if they are in front of the noun or behind it. Here are 4 examples:
un carro nuevo
(a brand new car)
un nuevo carro
(a different car)

un chico pobre
(a boy without money)
¡Pobre chico!
(Poor boy! (pity))

un profesor viejo
(an elderly teacher)
un viejo profesor
   (a long time teacher)

un presidente grande
(a tall/big president)
un gran presidente
(a great president)

la misma ciudad
(the same town)
la ciudad misma
(the very town)

Adjectives of Nationality

Adjectives of nationality whose masculine forms end in a consonant, (a consonant is any letter that's **not** *a*, *e*, *i*, *o*, or *u*) form the feminine by adding ***a***.

el hombre francés
la mujer frances**a**
 el profesor inglés
la profesora ingles**a**
el chico portugués
 la chica portugues**a**

Most adjectives of nationality have 4 forms. For example:
Masc. Singular -el chico mexican**o** (the Mexican boy)
Fem. Singular -la chica mexican**a** (the Mexican girl)
Masc. Plural -los chicos mexican**os** (the Mexican boys)
Fem. Plural -las chicas mexican**as** (the Mexican girls)

Other adjectives of nationality include:
 irlandés (Irish)   *alemán* (Gernan)
chino (Chinese)   *brasilero* (Brazilian)
ruso (Russian)   *japonés* (Japanese)
nigeriano (Nigerian)   *vietnamita* (Vietnamese)
Note: adjectives of nationality are not generally capitalized in Spanish except at the start of a sentence.

Exercise on Adjectives

Underline the adjective that most correctly describes the following nouns:

Noun   Adjective
1. el libro   (a)poca (b)muchas (c)amarillos (d)pequeño
2. las muchachas (a)altos (b)tímida (c)grande (d)simpáticas
3. el sombrero   (a)caro (b)bonita (c)rojas (d)pequeña
4. los gatos   (a)gordas (b)gordos (c)amarillas (d)activas
5. la mesa   (a)baja (b)morado (c)oscuro (d)blanco

Underline the adjective that most correctly describes the following nouns:

Noun   Adjective
1. la estudiante   (a)cómico (b)interesantes (c)atléticos (d)triste
2. los profesores (a)inteligentes (b)famosa (c)grande (d)trabajadoras
3. la rosa   (a)rojo (b)bonitas (c)verde (d)malo
4. el sol   (a)azules (b)brillantes (c)amarilla (d)brillante
5. la mosca   (a)chico (b)chicos (c)irritante (d)tonto

Translate the following:
1. Many students
2. Little time
3. Six pens
4. The new chairs
5. Few apples

Translate into Spanish the underlined phrases in the sentences that follow:

Mr. Jones is not *(1)* <u>a big man</u>, just five feet two inches, but the fair way in which he treated his employees marked him as *(2)* <u>a great man</u>.

Nate's family owned land, two car dealerships, and the biggest movie house in town but this *(3)* <u>poor boy</u> could never get a date. On the other hand, the *(4)* <u>poor boy</u> who lived in a trailer home and didn't have a penny to his name was loved by all the girls.

I just met my *(5)* <u>old friend</u>, Bill. Can you believe we both turn 25 this month! We met in the *(6)* <u>very street</u> we played as children.

Translate the following into Spanish:

1. The Russian winters
2. The Japanese women
3. The Brazilian car
4. The French schools
5. The English queen
6. The Irish sea

Solutions: Exercise on Adjectives

Underline the adjective that most correctly describes the following nouns:

Noun   Adjective
1. el libro   (a)poca (b)muchas
                          (c)amarillos (d)<u>pequeño</u>
2. las muchachas (a)altos (b)tímida (c)grande
(d)<u>simpáticas</u>
3. el sombrero   (a)<u>caro</u> (b)bonita (c)rojas
(d)pequeña
4. los gatos   (a)gordas (b)<u>gordos</u>
(c)amarillas (d)activas
5. la mesa   (a)<u>baja</u> (b)morado (c)oscuro
(d)blanco

Underline the adjective that most correctly describes the following nouns:

Noun   Adjective
1. la estudiante   (a)cómico (b)interesantes

(c)atléticos (d)<u>triste</u>

2. los profesores   (a)<u>inteligentes</u> (b)famosa
(c)grande (d)trabajadoras
3. la rosa   (a)rojo (b)bonitas (c)<u>verde</u>
(d)malo
4. el sol   (a)azules (b)brillantes
(c)amarilla (d)<u>brillante</u>
5. la mosca   (a)chico (b)chicos (c)<u>irritante</u>
(d)tonto

Translate the following:

6. muchos estudiantes
7. poco tiempo
8. Seis plumas
9. las sillas nuevas
10. Pocas manzanas

Translate into Spanish the underlined phrases in the sentences that follow:

Mr. Jones is not *(1)* a big man (hombre grande), just five feet two inches, but the fair way in which he treated his employees marked him as *(2)* a great man(gran hombre).

Nate's family owned land, two car dealerships, and the biggest movie house in town but this *(3)* poor boy (pobre chico) could never get a date. On the other hand, the *(4)* poor boy(chico pobre) who lived in a trailer home and didn't have a penny to his name was loved by all the girls.

I just met my *(5)* old friend (viejo amigo), Bill. Can you believe we both turn 25 this month! We met in the *(6)* very street (calle misma) we played as children.

Translate the following into Spanish:

7. Los inviernos rusos

8. Las mujeres japonesas

9. El carro brasilero

10. las escuelas francesas

11. la reina inglesa

12. el mar irlandés

Clothing and Colors

Objective: Enable the student to describe clothing worn in spring, summer, fall and winter.

Method: Accurately say and write the clothing and colors listed below.

Outcome: Produce 4 clothing shopping lists, 2 for males and 2 for females. Each one is dressed appropriately for a different season.

Clothing

bathing suit	el traje de baño
belt	el cinturón
blouse	la blusa
boots	las botas
cap	la cachucha, la gorra
clothes	la ropa
coat	el abrigo
dress	el vestido
ear muffs	las orejeras
gloves	los guantes
handbag	la bolsa
hat	el sombrero
jacket	la chaqueta
jeans	los jeans, los vaqueros
necktie	la corbata

pajamas	el pijama
pants	pantalones
raincoat	el impermeable
scarf	la bufanda
shirt	la camisa
short pants	pantalones cortos
skirt	la falda
slippers	las chanclas, las sandalias
flip-flops	las chanclas
socks	los calcetines
suit	el traje
shoes	los zapatos
sun glasses	las gafas de sol, los anteojos de sol
sweater	el suéter, la sudadera
swim trunk	el bañador
T-shirt	la camiseta

Colors

black	negro/a
blue	azul
brown	marrón, café
gray	gris
green	verde
orange	anaranjado/a
pink	rosado/a

purple	morado/a
red	rojo/a
white	blanco/a
yellow	amarillo/a

Seasons

Spring	la primavera
Summer	el verano
Fall	el otoño
Winter	el invierno
season	la estación

Sample Describing What You Are Wearing

Yo llevo una cacucha gris, una camiseta negra y blanca, pantalones verdes, los calcetines blancos y zapatos negros.
(I am wearing a gray cap, a black and white T-shirt, green pants, white socks, and black shoes.)

Sample Describing What a Classmate is Wearing

Christina lleva una blusa rosada y azul, los jeans, una bolsa café, y zapatos cafés.
(Christina is wearing a pink and blue blouse, jeans, a brown handbag and brown shoes.)

Exercise: Clothing and Colors

Produce 4 clothing shopping lists, 2 for males and 2 for females. Each one is dressed appropriately for a different season. Give *a color for each clothing item* you select.

Sample list

Nombre: Anita   *Estación*: la primavera

Ropa:
--un impermeable amarillo
--los jeans
--una sudadera roja
--botas negras
--una camiseta blanca

--un cinturón negro

A

Nombre: Esteban   *Estación*: la primavera
Ropa:
--
--
--
--
--
--

B

Nombre: Paulina   *Estación*: el verano

Ropa:

--

--

--

--

--

--

C

Nombre: Juan   *Estación*: El otoño

Ropa:

--

--

--

--

--

--

D

Nombre: Erica   *Estación*: el invierno

Ropa:

--

--

--

--

--

--

Oral Exercise: Clothing and Colors
Have students pair off and practice for about
10 minutes saying out loud what they are
wearing and what their partner is wearing.
After this, ask for volunteers to participate in
a whole class exercise.

Solutions to Exercise: Clothing and Colors

Answers will vary from student to student. Emphasize noun-adjective agreement and accuracy of pronunciation and spelling.

Solutions to Oral Exercise: Clothing and Colors

Help with pronunciation accuracy and noun-adjective agreement where needed.

Part 7

Prepositions, Possessives, Demonstratives, Articles

Using Prepositions and Prepositional Phrases to Tell where People and Objects are Located

Objective: Learn what prepositions and prepositional phrases are and how they are used.

Method: Practice written and/or oral exercises.

Outcome: Demonstrate mastery by correctly completing exercises that follow on prepositions and prepositional phrases. problems.

Definition

In English some common prepositions are: under, over, with, and beside. All of these words are prepositions or special words showing a relationship between two or more elements in a sentence. A prepositional phrase has the same function. For example

- *El gato está **debajo de** la mesa*. (The cat is **under** the table).

Here, *debajo de* (under) shows the relationship between the cat and the table.

The following 22-item list is made up of the more common prepositions and prepositional phrases that apply to the physical location of people and objects:

afuera (outside)
al lado de (next to)
a la derecha de (to the right of)
a la izquierda de (to the left of)
al cabo de (at the end of)
al exterior de (on the outside of)
a lo largo de (alongside)
cerca de (near to)
debajo de (underneath, under)
delante de (in front of)
dentro de (inside of)
detrás de (behind)
encima de (on top of)
enfrente de (opposite, facing)
En medio de (in the middle of)
entre (among, between)
frente a (opposite, facing)
fuera de (outside)
junto a (next to)
lejos de (far from)
más allá (beyond)
todo derecho (straight ahead)
todo recto (straight ahead)
rodeado de (surrounded by (people))

Exercise: Prepositions and Prepositional Phrases

Translate the following sentences intoSpanish:

1. The dog is among 6 cats.
2. The road is alongside the beach.
3. The city is beyond the big lake.
4. The gym is near to my house.
5. They are far from home.
6. The library is to the right of the office.
7. The old man is surrounded by many friends.
8. The yellow cars are in front of the garage.
9. Susanna and I are inside the restaurant.
10. The school is facing the supermarket.
11. The student is outside of the classroom .
12. The wall is behind the blackboard.
13. The man is to the left of the woman.
14. Two boxes are on top of the bed.
15. John is outside the cinema.
16. The offices are opposite the cafeteria.
17. The flowers are in the middle of the room.
18. The book is next to the ruler.
19. The trees are at the end of the path.
20. The computers are on top of 4 tables.

Solution to Exercise: Prepositions and Prepositional Phrases

Translate the following sentences intoSpanish:

1. The dog is among 6 cats. El perro está entre seis gatos
2. The road is alongside the beach. El camino está al lado de la playa.
3. The city is beyond the big lake. La ciudad está más allá del lago.
4. The gym is near to my house. El gimnsaio está cerca de mi casa.
5. They are far from home. Ellos están lejos de la casa.
6. The library is to the right of the office. La biblioteca está a la derecha de la oficina.
7. The old man is surrounded by many friends. El hombre viejo está rodeado de muchos amigos.
8. The yellow cars are in front of the garage.Los carros amarillos están enfrente del garage.
9. Susanna and I are inside the restaurant. Susanna y yo estamos dentro del restaurant.
10. The school is facing the supermarket. La escuela está enfrente del supermercado.
11. The student is outside of the classroom . El estudiante está al exterior del salón de clase.
12. The wall is behind the blackboard. La pared está detrás del pizarrón.

13. The man is to the left of the woman. El hombre está a la izquierda de la mujer.

14. Two boxes are on top of the bed. Dos cajas están encima de la cama.

15. John is outside the cinema. John está al exterior del cine.

16. The offices are opposite the cafetería. Las oficinas están enfrente de la cafeteria.

17. The flowers are in the middle of the room. Las flores están en medio del cuarto.

18. The book is next to the ruler. El libro está junto a la regla.

19. The trees are at the end of the path. Los árboles están al cabo del sendero.

20. The computers are on top of 4 tables. Las computadores están encima de cuatro mesas.

Possessive Adjectives

Objective: Learn how possessive adjectives are applied to the nouns they describe.
Method: Practice written and/or oral exercises.
Outcome: Demonstrate mastery by correctly completing exercises that follow on possessive adjectives.

Possessive adjectives function exactly as they promise – they indicate ownership. The possessive adjectives are:

1. mi (s) = my
2. tu (s) = your (familiar)
3. su (s) = his/her/its
4. su (s) = your (formal)
5. nuestro, nuestra, nuestros, nuestras = our
6. vuestro, vuestra, vuestros, vuestras = your (Spain)
7. su (s) = their
8. su (s) = your

Possessive adjectives cannot stand alone. They always describe a noun. For example
– mi hermano (my brother)

A possessive adjective is singular if the noun it describes is singular. For example
-*tu carro* (your car)
but it is plural if the noun it describes is plural. For example

-tus carros (your cars)

The possessive adjective must be the same in number and gender as the thing or things possessed when we use *nuestro* and *vuestro*. For example

- *nuestro libro* (our book)
- *nuestros libros* (our books)
- *nuestra silla* (our chair)
- *nuestras sillas* (our chairs)
- *vuestro libro* (your book)
- *vuestros libros* (your books)
- *vuestra silla* (your chair)
- *vuestras sillas* (your chairs)

Su and *sus* have more than one possible meaning and if you want to make your meaning clear, follow this pattern:

su mochila: *la mochila de* él (his backpack)

la mochila de ella (her backpack)
la mochila de Ud. (your backpack)
la mochila de ellos (their backpack)
la mochila de ellas (their backpack)
la mochila de Uds. (your backpack)

sus mochilas: *las mochilas de* él (his backpacks)

las mochilas de ella (her backpacks)
las mochilas de Ud. (your backpacks)
las mochilas de ellos (their backpacks)
las mochilas de ellas (their backpacks)
las mochilas de Uds. (your backpacks)

To ask the question to whom something belongs, use *De quién + ser* or *De quienés+ ser*. For example:

-*¿De quién son las casas*? (Whose houses are they?)

-*¿De quienés es el libro*? (Whose book is it?)

Exercise: Possessive adjectives

Underline the matching noun for each of the
following possessive adjectives:

1. mi   (a) libro (b) perros (c) chicas
             (d) plumas
2. tus   (a) prima (b) pluma (c) pelota
             (d) canciones
3. su   (a) taco (b) ranas (c) dilemmas
             (d) carros
4. sus   (a) mano (b) coro (c) lapiz (d) burros
5. nuestros (a) mapa (b) bicicletas (c) puercos
             (d) primas
6. vuestra   (a) oso (b) abuelo (c) churros
             (d) hermana
7. nuestro   (a) chicos (b) vestido (c) camisa

             (d) lápices

8 mis   (a) carro (b) fotos (c) muchacho
             (d) peso
9. nuestras (a) papas (b) tios (c) amigas (d) mesa
10. sus   (a) mochila (b) botellas (c) ratero
             (d) cachucha
11. nuestro (a) corbata (b) cunada (c) pelo
             (d) tacos
12. vuestras (a) silla (b) bicicletas (c) zapatos
             (d) puerta

13. tu   (a) mochilas (b) radio (c) tía

             (d) gatos

Exercise: Fill in the Blanks with the Correct Form of the Possessive Adjective

1. _____ carros son verdes.
(nuestra, vuestras, nuestros, mios)

2. _____ primos son médicos.
(mis, tu, nuestro, mios)

3. Yo tengo_____ comidas en casa.
(nuestra, vuestras, nuestros, su)

4. _____ entrenador es de Los Angeles.
(mi, tus, nuestros, un)

5. _____ amigas juegan al tenis.
(nuestra, vuestros, nuestras, mias)

6.Es _____ perro, y no es de Mario.
(tu, tus, nuestra, vuestros)

7.Me gusta _____ clases de arte y español.
(los, vuestro, tu, mis)

8. _____ sol brilla.
(mis, vuestras, nuestro, mios)

9.El béisebol y el tenis son _____ deportes favoritos.
(su, vuestras, nuestras, mis)

10. _____ bisabuelos viven en Anaheim.
(nuestras, vuestros, mi, tu)

11. _____ guantes son negros.
(nuestra, vuestras, nuestros, su)

12. _____ pantalones son cortos.
(mi, sus, tu, vuestro)

Solution to Exercise: Possessive Adjectives

Underline the matching noun for each of the following possessive adjectives:

1. mi   (a) <u>libro</u> (b) perros (c) chicas (d) plumas

2. tus   (a) prima (b) pluma (c) pelota (d) <u>canciones</u>

3. su   (a) <u>taco</u> (b) ranas (c) dilemmas (d) carros

4. sus   (a) mano (b) coro (c) lápiz (d) <u>burros</u>

5. nuestros   (a) mapa (b) bicicletas (c) <u>puercos</u> (d) primas

6. vuestra   (a) oso (b) abuelo (c) churros (d) <u>hermana</u>

7. nuestro   (a) chicos (b) <u>vestido</u> (c) camisa (d) lápices

8. mis   (a) carro (b) <u>fotos</u> (c) muchacho (d) peso

9. nuestras   (a) <u>papas</u> (b) tios (c) amigas (d) mesa

10. sus   (a) mochila (b) <u>botellas</u> (c) ratero (d) cachucha

11. nuestro   (a) corbata (b) cunada (c) <u>pelo</u> (d) tacos

12. vuestras (a) silla (b) <u>bicicletas</u> (c) zapatos (d) puerta

13. tu   (a) mochilas (b) radio (c) tía (d) gatos

Solution to Exercise: Fill in the Blanks with the Correct Form of the Possessive Adjective

1. <u>Nuestros</u> carros son verdes.
(nuestra, vuestras, nuestros, mios)

2. <u>Mis</u> primos son médicos.

(mis, tu, nuestro, mios)
3. Yo tengo <u>vuestras</u> comidas en casa.
(nuestra, vuestras, nuestros, su)
4. <u>Mi</u> entrenador es de Los Angeles.
(mi, tus, nuestros, un)
5. <u>Nuestras</u> amigas juegan al tenis.
(nuestra, vuestros, nuestras, mias)
6.Es <u>tu</u> perro, y no es de Mario.
(tu, tus, nuestra, vuestros)
7.Me gusta <u>mis</u> clases de arte y español.
(los, vuestro, tu, mis)
8. <u>Nuestro</u> sol brilla.
(mis, vuestras, nuestro, mios)

9.El béisebol y el tenis son mis deportes favoritos.

(su, vuestras, nuestras, mis)
10. <u>Vuestros</u> bisabuelos viven en Anaheim.
(nuestras, vuestros, mi, tu)
11. <u>Nuestros</u> guantes son negros.
(nuestra, vuestras, nuestros, su)
12. <u>Sus</u> pantalones son cortos.
(mi, sus, tu, vuestro)

Possessive Pronouns

Objective: Learn how possessive pronouns are used.

Method: Practice written and/or oral exercises.

Outcome: Demonstrate mastery by correctly completing exercises that follow on possessive pronouns.

Possessive pronouns, like possessive adjectives, are used to show ownership.

The following table lists the possessive pronouns:

English Possessive Pronouns	Spanish Possessive Pronouns Masculine	Spanish Possessive PronounsFeminine
Mine	Mío Míos	Mía Mías
Yours (familiar)	Tuyo Tuyos	Tuya Tuyas
His/Hers	Suyo Suyos	Suya Suyas
Yours (formal)	Suyo Suyos	Suya Suyas
Ours	Nuestro Nuestros	Nuestra Nuestras
Yours (Spain)	Vuestro Vuestros	Vuestra Vuestras
Theirs	Suyo Suyos	Suya Suyas
Yours	Suyo Suyos	Suya Suyas

Fig. 19

Unlike possessive adjectives that have to be paired with a noun, possessive pronouns don't have to be paired with anything because they replace nouns.

The gender and number of the thing possessed drives the gender and number of the possessive pronoun. **The gender of the owner does not count!** For example, *la casa* (the house), is feminine and singular therefore the sentence:

-*La casa es nuestra.* (the house is ours).

Las casas is feminine and plural therefore the sentence:

-*Las casas son nuestras* (the houses are ours).

Similarly, *el libro* is masculine and singular therefore the sentence:

-*El libro es mío.* (The book is mine).

Los libros is masculine and plural therefore the sentence:

Los libros son míos. (The books are mine)

Other examples are:

-*La manzana es tuya.* (the apple is yours).

-*El vestido es tuyo.* (The dress is yours).

-*Los perros son suyos.* (the dogs are his).

-*Las bicicletas son vuestras.* (The bicycles are yours).

Exercise: Possessive Pronouns

Fill in the blanks with the best choice of the possessive pronoun:

1. La mochila es _____ .
(a) suya (b) nuestros (c) tuyo (d) vuestras

2. Los libros son _____ .

(a) vuestro (b) nuestras (c) míos (d) tuyas

3. Las corbatas _____ son azules.

(a) vuestro (b) nuestras (c) míos (d) tuyos

4. El primo _____ es dentista.

(a) tuyos (b) nuestras (c) mío (d) suya

5. La ensalada _____ es deliciosa.

(a) nuestros (b) nuestra (c) mío (d) vuestras

6. El perro grande no es _____ .

(a) suyas (b) suyo (c) mía (d) nosotras

7. Las perlas negras son _____ .

(a) míos (b) suya (c) tuya (d) vuestras

8. Los sombreros son _____ .

(a) tuyas (b) nuestro (c) suyos (d) mío

9. La motocicleta _____ no sirve.

(a) tuyo (b) nuestro (c) vuestras (d) mía

10. El papel amarillo es_____ .

(a) nuestra (b) suyo (c) vuestra (d) míos

11. Los mapas _____.
(a) suyos (b) nuestras (c) tuyas (d) vuestro
12. El planeta _____ es precioso.
(a) tuyos (b) vuestra (c) tuya (d) nuestro
13 . La blusa _____ es roja y verde.

(a) suya (b) mías (c) vuestras (d) nuestras

14 . Los borradores _____ están aquí.

(a) nuestras (b) suyos (c) tuyas (d) vuestro

15. La camiseta _____ está mohada.

(a) suyos (b) nuestro (c) tuyo (d) vuestra
16. Los problemas_____ son grandes.
(a) vuestros (b) nuestras (c) suyas (d) vuestra

17. El periódico _____ no tiene sidoku.

(a) tuya (b) tuyos (c) suyos (d) mío
18. Las tortas _____ son de carne asada.
(a) vuestra (b) nuestras (c) tuyos (d) nuestros
19. El apartamento _____ es pequeño.
(a) tuya (b) tuyo (c) tuyos (d) tuyas
20. La ciudad es _____.
(a) nuestra (b) vuestros (c) suyas (d) tuyos
21. Los boletos son _____ .
(a) suyas (b) suyos (c) nuestras (d) vuestras

Solution to Exercise: Possessive Pronouns

Fill in the blanks with the best choice of the possessive pronoun:

1. La mochila es <u>suya</u>.
(a) suya (b) nuestros (c) tuyo (d) vuestras

2. Los libros son <u>míos</u>.

(a) vuestro (b) nuestras (c) míos (d) tuyas

3. Las corbatas <u>nuestras</u> son azules.

(a) vuestro (b) nuestras (c) míos (d) tuyos

4. El primo <u>mío</u> es dentista.

(a) tuyos (b) nuestras (c) mío (d) suya

5. La ensalada <u>nuestra</u> es deliciosa.

(a) nuestros (b) nuestra (c) mío (d) vuestras

6. El perro grande no es <u>suyo</u>.

(a) suyas (b) suyo (c) mía (d) nosotras

7. Las perlas negras son <u>vuestras</u>.

(a) míos (b) suya (c) tuya (d) vuestras

8. Los sombreros son <u>suyos</u>.

(a) tuyas (b) nuestro (c) suyos (d) mío

9. La motocicleta <u>mía</u> no sirve.

(a) tuyo (b) nuestro (c) vuestras (d) mía

10. El papel amarillo es <u>suyo</u>.

(a) nuestra (b) suyo (c) vuestra (d) míos

11. Los mapas suyos.
(a) suyos (b) nuestras (c) tuyas (d) vuestro
12. El planeta nuestro es precioso.
(a) tuyos (b) vuestra (c) tuya (d) nuestro
13 . La blusa suya es roja y verde.

(a) suya (b) mías (c) vuestras (d) nuestras

14 . Los borradores suyos están aquí.

(a) nuestras (b) suyos (c) tuyas (d) vuestro

15 . La camiseta vuestra está mohada.

(a) suyos (b) nuestro (c) tuyo (d) vuestra
16 . Los problemas vuestros son grandes.
(a) vuestros (b) nuestras (c) suyas (d) vuestra

17 . El periódico mío no tiene sidoku.

(a) tuya (b) tuyos (c) suyos (d) mío
18 . Las tortas nuestras son de carne asada.
(a) vuestra (b) nuestras (c) tuyos (d) nuestros
19 . El apartamento tuyo es pequeño.
(a) tuya (b) tuyo (c) tuyos (d) tuyas
20 . La ciudad es nuestra.
(a) nuestra (b) vuestros (c) suyas (d) tuyos
21 . Los boletos son suyos.
(a) suyas (b) suyos (c) nuestras (d) vuestras

Demonstrative Adjectives

Objective: Learn how demonstrative adjectives are applied to the nouns they describe.

Method: Practice written and/or oral exercises.

Outcome: Demonstrate mastery by correctly completing exercises that follow on demonstrative adjectives.

Here is a table of the demonstrative adjectives in Spanish along with their English meanings:

Singular	Masculine	Feminine	Plural	Masculine	Feminine
this	este	esta	these	estos	estas
that	ese	esa	those	esos	esas
that (way over there)	aquel	aquella	Those (way over there)	aquellos	aquellas

Fig. 20

The Spanish verb *demonstrar* means *to show* or *point out*. Demonstrative adjectives are used to point out this or that person, this or that place, or this or that thing.

Demonstrative adjectives agree in number and gender with the nouns they describe. For example

-*esta mochila* (this backpack.) *Mochila* is a feminine singular noun so its demonstrative adjective, *esta*, is also feminine and singular.

-*estas mochilas* (these backpacks.) *Mochilas* is a feminine plural noun so its demonstrative adjective, *estas*, is also feminine and plural.

-*este libro* (this book.) *Libro* is a masculnnine singular noun so its demonstrative adjective, *este*, is also masculine and singular.

-*estos libros* (these books.) *Libros* is a masculine plural noun so its demonstrative adjective, *estos*, is also masculine and plural.

A demonstrative adjective is more specific than the definite article (the), or the indefinite article (a/an, some). For example:

-*el carro* (the car)

-*un carro* (a car)

but
-*este carro* (this car)
To put this in context: *El carro de Raul es bueno, hay* *unos* *carros que son mejor, pero prefiero* **este** *carro rojo*. (Raul's car is good, there are some cars that are better, but I prefer this red car.)

Demonstrative adjectives are used to tell the location of a person, place or thing with relation to the speaker.
Este and all its forms indicate nearness to the speaker.
Ese and all its forms indicate middle distance from the speaker and listener.
Aquel and all its forms indicate greater distance from the speaker and listener.
Examples are:
-**Esta** *chica es alta*. (This girl (next to me) is tall.

-**Esa** *chica es cómica*. (That girl (a short distance away) is funny.)

-**Aquella** *chica es atlética*. (That girl (way over there) is athletic.)
Este, ese, aquel and all their forms not

only refer to distance but also to time. For example:

- *Voy a recordar este día pero aquellos años de mi niñez, yo recuerdo más.* (I time) but those years (much further away in time) of my childhood I remember most.)

Exercises: Demonstrative Adjectives

Fill in the blanks with the best choice of the demonstrative adjective:

Near to the speaker:
1. No nos gustan _____ peras.
(a) aquellos (b) esas (c) estas (d) estos
2. Los jueves nado en _____ piscina.
(a) aquella (b) esta (c) estas (d) estos
3. _____ vestidos son feos.
(a) estos (b) aquellos (c) esos (d) este
4. Les gustan _____ pantalones.
(a) esas (b) aquellos (c) estos (d) este

Near to the listener:
5. Voy a comer _____ pizza sabrosa.
(a) aquel (b) este (c) aquella (d) esa

6. Te gusta _____ cinturón rojo.

(a) este (b) aquella (c) estas (d) ese
7. Compro dos libras de _____ mangos.
(a) estos (b) esos (c) aquellos (d) ese
8. Prefieren _____ caballo blanco.
(a) ese (b) esa (c) aquel (d) este

Far away from speaker and listener:
9. _____ calles son peligrosas.
(a) esas (b) aquellas (c) aquella (d) estas
10. _____ carros son negros.
(a) estos (b) aquellas (c) aquellos (d) esos

11. Ella bebió _____ botella de agua.

(a) aquellas (b) esa (c) esta (d) aquella

12. ¿Quién es _____ chica guapa?

(a) esta (b) aquella (c) aquel (d) esa

Translate into Spanish

Near to the speaker:
1. This rose =
2. These shoes =
3. These boys =
4. This book =

Near to the listener:
5. Those girls =
6. That video =
7. Those pencils =
8. That cat =

Far away from speaker and listener:
9. That man =
10. Those houses =
11. That lamp =
12. These classes =

Solutions to Exercises: Demonstrative Adjectives

Fill in the blanks with the best choice of the demonstrative adjective:

Near to the speaker:
1. No nos gustan <u>estas</u> peras.
(a) aquellos (b) esas (c) estas (d) estos
2. Los jueves nado en <u>esta</u>　 piscina.
(a) aquella (b) esta (c) estas (d) estos
3. <u>Estos</u> vestidos son feos.
(a) estos (b) aquellos (c) esos (d) este
4. Les gustan <u>estos</u> pantalones.
(a) esas (b) aquellos (c) estos (d) este

Near to the listener:
5. Voy a comer <u>esa</u> pizza sabrosa.
(a) aquel (b) este (c) aquella (d) esa

6. Te gusta <u>ese</u> cinturón rojo.

(a) este (b) aquella (c) estas (d) ese
7. Compro dos libras de <u>esos</u> mangos.
(a) estos (b) esos (c) aquellos (d) ese
8. Prefieren <u>ese</u> caballo blanco.
(a) ese (b) esa (c) aquel (d) este

Far away from speaker and listener:
9. <u>Aquellas</u> calles son peligrosas.
(a) esas (b) aquellas (c) aquella (d) estas
10. <u>Aquellos</u> carros son negros.

(a) estos (b) aquellas (c) aquellos (d) esos

11.Ella bebió aquella botella de agua.

(a) aquellas (b) esa (c) esta (d) aquella

12.¿ Quién es aquella chica guapa?

(a) esta (b) aquella (c) aquel (d) esa

Translate into Spanish

Near to the speaker:
1. This rose = esta rosa
2. These shoes = estos zapatos
3. These boys = estos chicos
4. This book = este libro

Near to the listener:
5. Those girls = esas chicas
6. That video = ese video

7. Those pencils = estos lápices

8. That cat = ese gato

Far away from speaker and listener:
9. That man = aquel hombre
10. Those houses = aquellas casas

11.That lamp = aquella lámpara

12. These classes = aquellas clases

Demonstrative pronouns

Objective: Learn how demonstrative pronouns are used.

Method: Practice written and/or oral exercises.

Outcome: Demonstrate mastery by correctly completing exercises that follow on demonstrative pronouns.

Here is a table of the demonstrative pronouns in Spanish along with their English meanings:

Singular	Masculine	Feminine	Plural	Masculine	Feminine
this	éste	ésta	these	éstos	éstas
that	ése	ésa	those	ésos	ésas
that (way over there)	aquél	aquélla	those (way over there)	aquéllos	aquéllas

Fig. 21

245

Demonstrative pronouns bear close resemblance to demonstrative adjectives. The difference in form is the accent mark over the

é in all of the demonstrative pronouns.

Like all pronouns, demonstrative pronouns stand in place of a noun. For example

-*Esta pluma es roja pero **ésa** es amarilla*. (This pen is red but that one is yellow.)

-*Esos hombres son serios pero **aquéllos** son*

cómicos. (Those men are serious but those over there are funny.)
In the first example, *pluma*, pen, is replaced by *esa*, (that one) which refers back to the term *pluma* used in the first part of the sentence.
In the second example, *hombres* (men) is replaced by *aquellos*, (those over there) which refers back to the term *hombres* used in the first part of the sentence.

There are **3 additional demonstrative pronouns**. They are:

esto
eso
aquello

Unlike the other demonstrative pronouns, they are neuter, neither masculine nor feminine. They are used when we refer to an abstraction, a situation, or to an object for which we don't have a name.

For example:

- *Aquello es bueno* (That is good.)

- *Eso no es difícil de hacer* (That is not hard to do.)

-*¿Mamá, qué es esto?* (Mom, what is this?)

Es una corbata mi hija. (It's a necktie, my daughter.)

Exercise: Demonstrative Pronouns

Fill in the blanks with the correct choice of the demonstrative pronoun:

1. Este lago es más limpio que _____.

(a)) áquel (b) ésas (c) esta

2. Estas tiendas son más pequeñas que

_____.

(a) esta (b) (c) ésas (c) aquéllos

3. Estas vacas son más gordas que _____.

(a)) áquellas (b) ésos (c) esta

4. No me digas _____ de mi primo John.

(a)) áquel (b) éste (c) esto

5. ¿Dibujas tú con ese lápiz o _____?

(a) eso (b) ésa (c) aquél

6. Sofia llevó _____ a sus estudiantes.

(a)) aquel (b) aquello (c) ésa

7. Aquella leche es más pura que _____.

(a)) este (b) ésa (c) aquella

8. Aquellas piedras son más duras que

_____.

(a)) aquéllos (b) ésas (c) esta

9. Esta mujer es más seria que _____.

(a) aquellos (b) ésa (c) estas

10. Aquellos hospitales son más lejos que
_____.

(a)) aquel (b) ésos (c) ésta

11. Estos lápices son más largos que
_____.

(a) éstas (b) (c) ésas (c) aquéllos

12. Aquel niño es más tranqilo que _____.

(a)) éste (b) ésta (c) aquélla

13. Estas niñas son más trabajadoras que
_____.

(a) ésas (b) éstos (c) aquellas

14. Este hombre es mi padre y _____ es mi
tío. (a) aquel (b) ésa (c) ése

15. Aquella joya es de Cuba y _____ es de
Jamaica.

(a)) ésta (b) aquello (c) esa

16. Estas pelotas son mejores que _____.
(a) eso (b) éstos (c) aquéllas

17. Esas sillas son más pesadas que _____.

(a)) aquéllos (b) éstas (c) estos

18. Aquellos televisores son más caros que
_____.

(a) aquellos (b) ésa (c) éstos

19. Aquel soldado es más alto que _____.

(a) éste (b) esas (c) estas

20. Esta puerta es más ancha que _____.

(a) esos (b) ésas (c) estas

21. Estos camiones son peores que_____.

 (a) éstas (b) esas (c) aquéllos

22. Esos carros son menos baratos que_____.

(a) éstos (b) esas (c) aquéllas

Solution to Exercise: Demonstrative Pronouns

Fill in the blanks with the correct choice of the demonstrative pronoun:

1. Este lago es más limpio que <u>áquel</u>.

(a)) áquel (b) ésas (c) esta

2. Estas tiendas son más pequeñas que <u>ésas</u>.

(a) esta (b) (c) ésas (c) aquéllos

3. Estas vacas son más gordas que <u>áquellas</u>.

(a)) áquellas (b) ésos (c) esta
4. No me digas <u>esto</u> de mi primo John.

(a)) áquel (b) éste (c) esto

5. ¿Dibujas tú con ese lápiz o <u>aquél</u>?

(a) eso (b) ésa (c) aquél

6. Sofia llevó <u>aquello</u> a sus estudiantes.

(a)) aquel (b) aquello (c) ésa

7. Aquella leche es más pura que <u>ésa</u>.

(a)) este (b) ésa (c) aquella

8. Aquellas piedras son más duras que <u>ésas</u>.

(a)) aquéllos (b) ésas (c) esta

9. Esta mujer es más seria que <u>ésa</u>.

(a) aquellos (b) ésa (c) estas

10. Aquellos hospitales son más lejos que ésos.

(a)) aquel (b) ésos (c) ésta

11. Estos lápices son más largos que aquéllos.

(a) éstas (b) (c) ésas (c) aquéllos

12. Aquel niño es más tranqilo que éste.

(a)) éste (b) ésta (c) aquélla

13. Estas niñas son más trabajadoras que ésas.

(a) ésas (b) éstos (c) aquellas

14. Este hombre es mi padre y ése es mi tío.

(a) aquel (b) ésa (c) ése

15. Aquella joya es de Cuba y ésta es de Jamaica.

(a)) ésta (b) aquello (c) esa

16. Estas pelotas son mejores que aquéllas.

(a) eso (b) éstos (c) aquéllas

17. Esas sillas son más pesadas que éstas.

(a)) aquéllos (b) éstas (c) estos

18. Aquellos televisores son más caros que éstos.

(a) aquellos (b) ésa (c) éstos

19. Aquel soldado es más alto que éste.

(a) éste (b) esas (c) estas

20. Esta puerta es más ancha que ésa.

(a) esos (b) ésas (c) estas

21. Estos camiones son peores que aquéllos.

(a) éstas (b) esas (c) aquéllos

22. Esos carros son menos baratos que éstos.

(a) éstos (b) esas (c) aquéllas

The Definite and Indefinite Articles

Objective: Learn what definite articles and indefinite articles are and how they are used.
Method: Practice written and/or oral exercises.
Outcome: Demonstrate mastery by correctly completing exercises that follow on definite articles and indefinite articles.

This lesson introduces us to **the definite article** and **the indefinite article**. It will tell us what they are and how they are used.

The Definite Article

Figure 22 displays the definite articles in Spanish along with their English meaning:

	Singular	**Plural**
Masculine (the)	*el* El pavo El cuarto	*los* Los pavos Los cuartos
Feminine (the)	*la* la planta la cama	*las* las plantas las camas

Fig. 22

There are four forms of the Spanish definite article:
   el, la, los, las.
They all mean "the" in English.

   The definte article has 7 principal uses.
   1. To indicate a definite person or
      thing.
      -*El* carro es viejo. (The car is old.)
      -*La* muchacha es seria. (The girl is

serious.)

*-**Los** zapatos de mi hermano.* (My brother's shoes.)

*-**Las** enfermeras son excelentes.* (The nurses are excellent.)

2. The article marks a noun as either masculine or feminine. *El* marks a noun as masculine and *la* marks a noun as feminine. For example

-el lápiz (the pencil)

-la mano (the hand)

To take this a step further, many nouns of Greek origin are masculine even though they end with the letter *a*.
For example
-el problema (the problem)
-el dilema (the dilemma)
-el mapa (the map)
-el planeta (the planet)

Although many masculine nouns end with the letter *o* and many feminine nouns end with the letter *a*, in some cases this is not true. Without their articles, it might be hard for a beginner to guess the gender of some of the nouns above.

When learning new vocabulary, learn your nouns along with their definite articles. This is important since adjectives and pronouns often change to match a noun's gender.

3.The definite article matches the gender and number of its noun (See *Fig. 22*). If the noun is masculine and singular (*pavo*) its article must also be masculine and singular (*el pavo*). Similarly, if the noun is masculine and plural (*pavos*) its article must also be masculine and plural (*los pavos*). The same principle applies to feminine nouns (See *Fig. 22*).

4. The definite article is used to indicate when a noun is used in a general sense or to talk about a class of things. For example

-*Marisela evita el queso*. (Marisela avoids cheese). This means all cheeses not just one or two types.

-*Las cercas son útiles*. (Fences are useful). Here too we refer to *fences* as a category.

Note that the Spanish definite article does

not normally carry over into its English translation, *the*, in these cases:

5. It is used to talk about parts of the body. For example

-*¿Te duele la pierna?* (does your leg hurt?)

6. In **dates and time of day**. For example

-*El primero de mayo.* (May first.)

-*Son las tres y media.* (It's 3:30)

7. The definite article is used with **titles**, except when addressing the title holder directly. For example

-*el presidente Obama* (President Obama)

-*la doctora Rojas* (doctor Rojas)

-*el señor Machado* (Mr. Machado)

But

-*¿Cómo está usted, señor Machado?*

(How are you, Mr. Machado?)

The Indefinite Article

Below is a table of the indefinite articles in Spanish along with their English meanings:

	Singular	Plural
Masculine	***un***(a, an) un amigo un sello	***unos*** (some) unos amigos unos sellos
Feminine	***una***(a, an) una puerta una chica	***unas*** (some) unas puertas unas chicas

Fig. 23

Usage

1. The indefinite article is used with reference to persons, animals, places, or things that are not specifically identified. Let's contrast the definite articles with the indefinite article to illustrate this point:

-*el* *sello* (the stamp that I may have in my hand or am looking at directly.)

 but

un *sello* (a stamp that may be anywhere or is being referred to in an abstract sense.)

The Spanish indefinite articles agree in number and gender with the nouns they describe. See *Fig. 23*. For example, *puerta* is a singular feminine noun so it can only take the singular feminine indefinite article *una*.

-*una* *puerta* (a door)

The noun *puertas* is a plural, feminine noun so it can only take the plural, feminine indefinite article, *unas*.

-*unas* *puertas* (some doors)

The same pattern applies to Spanish indefinite articles that are masculine.

2. The indefinite article is usually **not used**:
 In front of nouns of nationality, religion, occupation, or political association, when preceded by *ser*. For example

-*Es francés.* (He is a Frenchman.)

-*Es comunista.* (She is a communist.)
-*Ella es profesora.* (She is a teacher.)
But
When these nouns are described, the indefinite article is used. For example

*-Es **un** francés de fama cientifica.* (He is a
Frenchman of scientific fame)
*-Ella es **una** profesora muy paciente.* (She is
a very patient teacher.)

3. In front of nouns coming after the following
words:

Sin, cierto, tal, que, cien, mil
For example
-¡Que hombre!. (What a man!)
-Mil veces. (a thousand times)

Exercise: Apply the Correct Form of the Definite or Indefinite Article to its Noun

Fill in each blank cell with the indicated definite or indefinite Spanish article.

English Definite/Indefinite Article	Supply Spanish Definite or Indefinite Article	Spanish Noun
1. the		retrato
2. a		caballo
3. the		examen
4. a		aldea
5. some		meses
6. a		lago
7. the		invitación
8. the		tierra
9. some		tazas
10. a		tema
11. the		iglesia
12. some		bomberos
13. the		lugar
14. some		crucigramas
15. a		video

Fig. 24

16. the		fotos
17. the		chico
18. some		francesas
19. the		correo
20. some		camionetas
21. some		cumbres
22. a		sol
23. a		caridad
24. the		pájaros
25. a		zapato
26. some		bibliotecas
27. the		ciudad
28. the		revoluciones
29. a		bandera
30. the		amor
31. the		pan

Fig. 24 (cont'd)

Solution to Exercise: Apply the Correct Form of the Definite or Indefinite Article to its Noun

Fill in each blank cell with the indicated definite or indefinite Spanish article

English Definite/Indefinite Article	Supply Spanish Definite or Indefinite Article	Spanish Noun
1. the	**el**	retrato
2. a	**un**	caballo
3. the	**el**	examen
4. a	**una**	aldea
5. some	**unos**	meses
6. a	**un**	lago
7. the	**la**	invitación
8. the	**la**	tierra
9. some	**unas**	tazas
10. a	**un**	tema
11. the	**la**	iglesia
12. some	**unos**	bomberos
13. the	**el**	lugar
14. some	**unos**	crucigramas
15. a	**un**	video
16. the	**las**	fotos

Fig. 25

17. the	**el**	chico
18. some	**unas**	francesas
19. the	**el**	correo
20. some	**unas**	camionetas
21. some	**unas**	cumbres
22. a	**un**	sol
23. a	**una**	caridad
24. the	**los**	pájaros
25. a	**un**	zapato
26. some	**unas**	bibliotecas
27. the	**la**	ciudad
28. the	**las**	revoluciones
29. a	**una**	bandera
30. the	**el**	amor
31. the	**el**	pan

Fig. 25 (cont'd)

Part 8

A Pronunciation Guide

A Pronunciation Guide to High Frequency Spanish Words

The word list that follows is a simple phonetic guide to the pronunciation of 188 high frequency Spanish words. This list is the result of a combination of several high frequency Spanish word lists and the author's own teaching experience.

Convention

In a word of two or more syllables, the stressed vowel is capped. Example: *necesito* = nay-say-sEe-tow.
The Spanish word is on the left, its pronunciation is on the right.

a	ah
abajo	ah-bA-ho
agua	Ag-wah
ahí	ah-yE
ahora	ah-Aura
al	rhymes with "pal"

algo	Al-go
almuerzo	al-mwEr-zoe
alto	Al-toe
a veces	ah bAy-ces
alguien	alg-yEn
alguna	al-gU-nah
allí	ah-yE
antes	Ant-ace
amigo	ah-mI-go
aquí	ah-kEy
así	ah-sEa
antes	Ant-ace
aún	ah-wOOOn
bien	bee-yEn
bonito	boh-knEE-toe
buen	bwEn
bueno	bwEn-o
cada	kAh-dah

casa	kA-sah
cena	sAy-nah
chiquito	chi-kEy-toe
cierto	see-Air-toe
claro	klAr-oh
como	kO-moe
con	cOne
conmigo	kon-mE-go
contigo	kon-tEa-go
crees	crAy-ace
creo	crAy-oh
cuando	kwAn-doe
de	day
debajo	day-bAh-hoe
debe	dAy-bay
decir	day-sEEr

del	dale
desde	dAys-day
después	days-pwAce (A as in f*a*ce)
día	dEE-ah
dice	dEE-say
dijo	dEE-hoe
dinero	dee-nAy-roe
donde	dOn-day
desayuno	days-ah-yOu-know
dos	dose
el	ale
ella	Aya (A as in b*ay*)
en	("en" same as *ain* in **ain**t)
es	ace
esta	ace-tAh (A as in *a*loft)
estoy	ace-tOy

estado	ace-tAh-doe
estar	ace-stAr
era	Ay-rah
eres	Ay-race
esa	Ace-ah
ese	Ace-say
están	ace-stAn
falso	fAl-soe (*Al* as in p**al**)
feliz	fay-lEase
fue	fway
fueron	fwAy-ron
fui	foo-EE
fuimos	foo-EE-moose
fuera	foo-Era
gente	Aint-ay
grande	grAnd-ay

gracias	grA-see-ass
gusta	gOOse-tah
hace	Ah-say
hacer	ah-zEr
haber	ah-bEar
había	ah-bEE-ya
han	ann
has	ass
hasta	Ass-tah
hay	eye
hecho	Ay-cho
hermana	air-mAn-ah
hermano	air-mAn-oh
hora	aura
hoy	oy
importa	eem-pOOr-tah

ir	ear
Juan	wan
jugar	who-gAr
juego	wAy-go
jugo	whO-go
la	lah
las	lass
leer	lay-Air
les	lace
lo	low
luego	lwE-go
major	may-hOar
mal	(rhymes with pal)
mamá	ma-mAAh
manaña	man-yA-na
me	may

menor	may-nOr
menos	mAy-nos
mi	me
mil	meal
mis	meese
mismo	mEEs-mo
mira	mE-rah
mucho	mOO-cho
mujer	moo-hAir
muy	mOO-ee
nada	nA-dah
nadie	nAd-yea
naranja	nah-rAng-ha
necesito	nay-say-sEE-toe
niño	nIn-yo
niña	nIn-ya

nosotros	no-sO-tros
noche	nO-chay
nuestro	noo-Ace-tro
nunca	nOOn-kah
oir	owe-Eer
otro	Owe-troe
oye	O-yea
para	pA-rah
parte	pAr-tay
pasa	pAss-ah
pero	pAy-row
poco	pO-koh
poder	po-dAir
poquito	po-kEy-toe
por	pOOr
porque	poor-kAy
puede	pwAy-day
puedo	pwE-doe

que	kay
quien	key-Enn
quiere	key-Ay-ray
quiero	key-Ay-row
quizás	keys-Ass
razón	rah-sOn
raya	rAh-ya
regla	rAy-glah
ropa	roe-pAh
se	say
sea	sAy-ah
ser	sair
será	sair-Ah
si	see
siempre	see-Emp-pray
siento	see-En-toe

sin	seen
sobre	sEw-bray
solo	sO-low
son	sewn
soy	("o" matches *o* in m*o*le)
tal	(rhymes with *al* in p*al*)
también	tamb-yEn
tarde	tAr-day
te	tay
tener	ten-Air
tengo	tEng-oh
ti	tea
tiene	tea-Ay-nay
todo	tOe-doe
tres	trace
tu	too

una	OO-nah ("OO" as in m*oo*n)
uno	OO-no ("OO" as in m*oo*n)
usted	oost-Aid
va	bah
vamos	bA-mos
van	ban
ven	ben
veo	bAy-oh
ver	bare
verdad	bare-dAd
vez	base
vida	bEE-dah
viene	bee-Ay-nay
visto	bEEs-toe
voy	bOy ("O" has value as o in b*o*wl)

y	ee
ya	yah
yo	yoh

Part 9

Appendix A

Understanding how Names work in Conjugations

Spanish verbs follow patterns in the way they are conjugated whether they are regular verbs in the present tense like *tomar*, *comer*, and *vivir* or an irregular verb such as *ser*. These patterns continue in past tenses as illustrated by the verb *buscar*.

Take a careful look at all of the conjugated verbs, and you will notice symbols (* † +) in positions 3, 5, and 7 respictively. An explanation of what these symbols mean comes after you take a quick look at the conjugated verbs that follow.

Singular
1. yo tomo = I drink

2. tú tomas = you (fam.) drink

*3. él/ella toma = he/she/it drinks

4. usted toma = you (form.) drink

Plural

†5. nosotros tomamos = we drink

6. vosotros tomáis = you drink

+7.ellos/ellas toman = they drink.

 8. ustedes toman = you drink

<u>Singular</u>

1. yo como = I eat

2. tú comes = you (fam.) eat

*3. él/ella come = he/she/it eats.

 4. usted come = you (form.) eat
<u>Plural</u>

†5. nosotros comemos = we eat

6. vosotros coméis = you eat

+7.ellos/ellas comen = they eat.

8. ustedes comen = you eat

<u>Singular</u>

1. yo vivo = I live

2. tú vives = you (fam.) live

*3. él/ella vive = he/she/it lives

4.usted vive = you (form.) live

<u>Plural</u>

†5. nosotros vivimos = we live

6. vosotros vivís = you live

+7.ellos/ellas viven = they live

8. ustedes viven = you live

<u>Singular</u>
1. yo soy = I am

2. tú eres = you are (familiar)

*3. él/ella es = he/she/it is

 4. usted es = you are (formal)

<u>Plural</u>
†5. nosotros somos = we are
6. vosotros sois = you are
+7.ellos/ellas son = they are
 8. ustedes son = you are

Singular
1. yo busqué = I looked for
2.tú buscaste = you (familiar) looked for
*3. él/ella buscó = he/she/it looked for
4. usted buscó = you (formal) looked for
Plural
†5. nosotros/as buscamos = we looked for
6. vosotros/as buscasteis = you (Sp.) looked for
+7.ellos/as buscaron = they looked for
8. ustedes buscaron = you looked for

Key to Symbols in Conjugations Above

* = The name of 1 person or 1 thing can replace *él/ella* in position 3 above. Example: *John toma agua.* (John drinks water).

† = Whenever the phrase ...y yo (...and I) occurs, use the verb in position 5 above. Example: *Susie, Paula **y yo** tomamos agua.* (Susie Paula **and I** drink water).

+ = The name of 2 or more persons or 2 or more things can replace *ellos/ellas* in position 3 above. Example: *John y Anita toman agua.* (John drinks water). *Los gatos toman leche.* (The cats drink milk)

Note: These same conditions apply in positions 3, 5, and 7 for any fully conjugated Spanish verb in whatever tense.

Part 10

Appendix B

Your Feedback is Greatly Appreciated

For books of this type to attain their full potential, colaboration between author and user is cannot be overstated.

As the writer, I might be blind to this book's shortcomings because I've been very close to it for some time now.

I need your comments about what you found useful, what both positive and negative, so I can eliminate or strengthen weaker points and continue what's good. Please send your comments to: *griot1017@gmail.com*

Be fearless! Thanks.

Made in the USA
San Bernardino, CA
26 March 2015